The Wisdom of Life

ARTHUR SCHOPENHAUER

Translated by
T. Bailey Saunders

DOVER PUBLICATIONS, INC.
Mineola, New York

Bibliographical Note

This Dover edition, first published in 2004, is an unabridged republication of *The Wisdom of Life; Being the First Part of Arthur Schopenhauer's Aphorismen zur Lebensweisheit*, originally published in 1890 by Swan Sonnenschein & Co., Ltd., London.

Library of Congress Cataloging-in-Publication Data

Schopenhauer, Arthur, 1788–1860.
    [Aphorismen zur Lebensweisheit. English]
    The wisdom of life / Arthur Schopenhauer ; translated by T. Bailey Saunders.—
Dover ed.
      p. cm.
    Originally published: London : S. Sonnenschein & Co., 1890.
    ISBN-13: 978-0-486-43550-3 (pbk.)
    ISBN-10: 0-486-43550-4 (pbk.)
    1. Conduct of life. 2. Maxims. I. Saunders, T. Bailey (Thomas Bailey),
1860–1928. II. Title.

B3118.E5S34 2004
170'.44—dc22

2003065489

Manufactured in the United States by RR Donnelley
43550405   2015
www.doverpublications.com

Translator's Preface

SCHOPENHAUER is one of the few philosophers who can be generally understood without a commentary. All his theories claim to be drawn direct from the facts, to be suggested by observation, and to interpret the world as it is; and whatever view he takes, he is constant in his appeal to the experience of common life. This characteristic endows his style with a freshness and vigour which would be difficult to match in the philosophical writing of any country, and impossible in that of Germany. If it were asked whether there were any circumstances, apart from heredity, to which he owed his mental habit, the answer might be found in the abnormal character of his early education, his acquaintance with the world rather than with books, the extensive travels of his boyhood, his ardent pursuit of knowledge for its own sake and without regard to the emoluments and endowments of learning. He was trained in realities even more than in ideas; and hence he is original, forcible, clear, an enemy of all philosophic indefiniteness and obscurity; so that it may well be said of him, in the words of a writer in the "Revue Contemporaine," *ce n'est pas un philosophe comme les autres, c'est un philosophe qui a vu le monde.*

It is not my purpose, nor would it be possible within the limits of a prefatory note, to attempt an account of Schopenhauer's philosophy, to indicate its sources, or to suggest or rebut the objections which may be taken to it. M. Ribot, in his excellent little book,* has done all that is necessary in this direction. But the essays here presented need a word of explanation. It should be observed, and Schopenhauer himself is at pains to point out, that his system is like a citadel with a hundred gates: at whatever point you take it up, wherever you make your entrance, you are on the road to the centre. In this respect his writings resemble a series of essays composed in support of a single thesis; a circumstance which led him to insist, more emphatically even than most philosophers, that for a proper understanding of his system it was necessary to

---

*La Philosophie de Schopenhauer, par Th. Ribot.

read every line he had written. Perhaps it would be more correct to describe *Die Welt als Wille und Vorstellung* as his main thesis, and his other treatises as merely corollary to it. The essays in these volumes form part of the corollary; they are taken from a collection published towards the close of Schopenhauer's life, and by him entitled *Parerga una Paralipomena*, as being in the nature of surplusage and illustrative of his main position. They are by far the most popular of his works, and since their first publication in 1851 they have done much to build up his fame. Written so as to be intelligible enough in themselves, the tendency of many of them is towards the fundamental idea on which his system is based. It may therefore be convenient to summarise that idea in a couple of sentences; more especially as Schopenhauer sometimes writes as if his advice had been followed and his readers were acquainted with the whole of his work.

All philosophy is in some sense the endeavour to find a unifying principle, to discover the most general conception underlying the whole field of nature and of knowledge. By one of those bold generalisations which occasionally mark a real advance in science Schopenhauer conceived this unifying principle, this underlying unity, to consist in something analogous to that *will* which self-consciousness reveals to us. *Will* is, according to him, the fundamental reality of the world, the thing-in-itself; and its objectivation is what is presented in phenomena. The struggle of the will to realise itself evolves the organism, which in its turn evolves intelligence as the servant of the will. And in practical life the antagonism between the will and the intellect arises from the fact that the former is the metaphysical substance, the latter something accidental and secondary. And further, will is *desire*, that is to say, need of something; hence need and pain are what is positive in the world, and the only possible happiness is a negation, a renunciation of *the will to live.*

It is instructive to note, as M. Ribot points out, that in finding the origin of all things, not in intelligence, as some of his predecessors in philosophy had done, but in will, or the force of nature, from which all phenomena have developed, Schopenhauer was anticipating something of the scientific spirit of the nineteenth century. To this it may be added that in combating the method of Fichte and Hegel, who spun a system out of abstract ideas, and in discarding it for one based on observation and experience, Schopenhauer can be said to have brought down philosophy from heaven to earth.

In Schopenhauer's view the various forms of Religion are no less a product of human ingenuity than Art or Science. He holds, in effect, that all religions take their rise in the desire to explain the world; and that, in regard to truth and error, they differ, in the main, not by preach-

ing monotheism, polytheism or pantheism, but in so far as they recognise pessimism or optimism as the true description of life. Hence any
religion which looked upon the world as being radically evil appealed
to him as containing an indestructible element of truth. I have en-
deavoured to present his view of two of the great religions of the world
in the extract which comes in the third volume, and to which I have
given the title of *The Christian System*. The tenor of it is to show that,
however little he may have been in sympathy with the supernatural element, he owed much to the moral doctrines of Christianity and of
Buddhism, between which he traced great resemblance.

Of Schopenhauer, as of many another writer, it may be said that he
has been misunderstood and depreciated just in the degree in which he
is thought to be new; and that, in treating of the Conduct of Life, he is,
in reality, valuable only in so far as he brings old truths to remem-
brance. His name used to arouse, and in certain quarters still arouses,
a vague sense of alarm; as though he had come to subvert all the rules
of right thinking and all the principles of good conduct, rather than to
proclaim once again and give a new meaning to truths with which the
world has long been familiar. Of his philosophy in its more technical
aspects, as matter upon which enough, perhaps, has been written, no
account need be taken here, except as it affects the form in which he
embodies these truths or supplies the fresh light in which he sees them.
For whatever claims to originality his metaphysical theory may possess,
the chief interest to be found in his views of life is an affair of form
rather than of substance; and he stands in a sphere of his own, not because he sets new problems or opens up undiscovered truths, but in the
manner in which he approaches what has been already revealed.

He is not on that account less important; for the great mass of men
at all times requires to have old truths imparted as if they were new—
formulated, as it were, directly for them as individuals, and of special
application to their own circumstances in life. A discussion of human
happiness and the way to obtain it is never either unnecessary or un-
called for, if one looks to the extent to which the lives of most men fall
short of even a poor ideal, or, again, to the difficulty of reaching any
definite and secure conclusion. For to such a momentous inquiry as
this, the vast majority of mankind gives nothing more than a nominal
consideration, accepting the current belief whatever it may be, on authority, and taking as little thought of the grounds on which it rests as
a man walking takes of the motion of the earth. But for those who are
not indifferent—for those whose desire to fathom the mystery of existence gives them the right to be called thinking beings—it is just here,
in regard to the conclusion to be reached, that a difficulty arises, a difficulty affecting the conduct of life: for while the great facts of existence

are alike for all, they are variously appreciated, and conclusions differ, chiefly from innate diversity of temperament in those who draw them. It is innate temperament, acting on a view of the facts necessarily incomplete, that has inspired so many different teachers. The tendencies of a man's own mind—the Idols of the Cave before which he bows—interpret the facts in accordance with his own nature: he elaborates a system containing, perhaps, a grain of truth, to which the whole of life is then made to conform; the facts purporting to be the foundation of the theory, and the theory in its turn giving its own colour to the facts.

Nor is this error, the manipulation of facts to suit a theory, avoided in the views of life which are presented by Schopenhauer. It is true that he aimed especially at freeing himself from the trammels of previous systems; but he was caught in those of his own. His natural desire was to resist the common appeal to anything extramundane, anything outside or beyond life, as the basis of either hope or fear. He tried to look at life as it is; but the metaphysical theory on which his whole philosophy rests made it necessary for him, as he thought, to regard it as an unmixed evil. He calls our present existence an infinitesimal moment between two eternities, the past and the future, a moment, like the life of Plato's "Dwellers in the Cave," filled with the pursuit of shadows; where everything is relative, phenomenal, illusory, and man is bound in the servitude of ignorance, struggle and need, in the endless round of effort and failure. If you confine yourself, says Schopenhauer, only to some of its small details, life may indeed appear to be a comedy, because of the one or two bright spots of happy circumstance to be found in it here and there; but when you reach a higher point of view and a broader outlook, these soon become invisible, and Life, seen from the distance which brings out the true proportion of all its parts, is revealed as a tragedy—a long record of struggle and pain, with the death of the hero as the final certainty. How then, he asks, can a man make the best of his brief hour under the hard conditions of his destiny? What is the true Wisdom of Life?

Schopenhauer has no pre-conceived divine plan to vindicate; no religious or moral enthusiasm to give a roseate hue to some far-off event, obliging us in the end to think that all things work together for good. Let poets and theologians give play to imagination! he, at any rate, will profess no knowledge of anything beyond our ken. If our existence does not entirely fail of its aim, it must, he says, be *suffering*; for this is what meets us everywhere in the world, and it is absurd to look upon it as the result of chance. Still, in the face of all this suffering, and in spite of the fact that the uncertainty of life destroys its value as an end in itself, every man's natural desire is to preserve his existence; so that life is a blind, unreasoning force, hurrying us we know not whither. From his high metaphysical standpoint, Schopenhauer is ready to admit that there are many things in life which give a short satisfaction and blind us for the moment to the realities of existence,—pleasures as they may be called, in so far as they are a mode of *relief*; but that pleasure is not positive in its nature nor anything more than the negation of suffering, is proved by the fact that, if pleasures come in abundance, pain soon returns in the form of satiety; so that the sense of illusion is all that has been gained. Hence, the most a man can achieve in the way of welfare is a measure of relief from this suffering; and if people were prudent, it is at this they would aim, instead of trying to secure a happiness which always flies from them.

It is a trite saying that happiness is a delusion, a chimæra, the *fata morgana* of the heart; but here is a writer who will bring our whole conduct into line with it, as a matter of practice; making pain the positive groundwork of life, and a desire to escape it the spur of all effort. While most of those who treat of the conduct of life come at last to the conclusion, more or less vaguely expressed, that religion and morality form a positive source of true happiness, Schopenhauer does not professedly take this view; though it is quite true that the practical outcome of his remarks tends, as will be seen, to support it. His method is different: he does not direct the imagination to anything outside this present life as making it worth while to live at all; his object is to state the facts of existence as they immediately appear, and to draw conclusions as to what a wise man will do in the face of them.

In the practical outcome of Schopenhauer's ethics—the end and aim of those maxims of conduct which he recommends, there is nothing that is not substantially akin to theories of life which, in different forms, the greater part of mankind is presumed to hold in reverence. It is the premises rather than the conclusion of his argument which interest us as something new. The whole world, he says, with all its phenomena of change, growth and development, is ultimately the manifestation of Will—*Wille und Vorstellung*—a blind force conscious of itself only when it reaches the stage of intellect. And life is a constant self-assertion of this will, a long desire which is never fulfilled. Disillusion inevitably follows upon attainment, because the will, the thing-in-itself—in philosophical language, the *noumenon*—always remains as the permanent element; and with this persistent exercise of its claim, it can never be satisfied. So life is essentially suffering; and the only remedy for it is the freedom of the intellect from the servitude imposed by its master, the will.

The happiness a man can attain, is thus, in Schopenhauer's view, negative only; but how is it to be acquired? Some temporary relief, he says, may be obtained through the medium of Art; for in the appre-

hension of Art we are raised out of our bondage, contemplating objects
of thought as they are in themselves, apart from their relations to our
own ephemeral existence, and free from any taint of the will. This contemplation of pure thought is destroyed when Art is degraded from its
lofty sphere, and made an instrument in the bondage of the will. How
few of those who feel that the pleasure of Art transcends all others
could give such a striking explanation of their feeling!

But the highest ethical duty, and consequently the supreme endeavour after happiness, is to withdraw from the struggle of life, and so obtain release from the misery which that struggle imposes upon all, even
upon those who are for the moment successful. For as will is the inmost
kernel of everything, so it is identical under all its manifestations; and
through the mirror of the world a man may arrive at the knowledge of
himself. The recognition of the identity of our own nature with that of
others is the beginning and foundation of all true morality. For when a
man clearly perceives this solidarity of the will, there is aroused in him
a feeling of *sympathy* which is the main-spring of ethical conduct. This
feeling of sympathy must, in any true moral system, prevent our ob-
taining success at the price of others' loss. Justice, in this theory, comes
to be a noble, enlightened self-interest; it will forbid our doing wrong
to our fellow-man, because, in injuring him, we are injuring ourselves—our own nature, which is identical with his. On the other
hand, the recognition of this identity of the will must lead to commis-
eration—a feeling of sympathy with our fellow-sufferers—to acts of
kindness and benevolence, to the manifestation of what Kant, in the
Metaphysic of Ethics, calls the only absolute good, *the good will*. In
Schopenhauer's phraseology, the human will, in other words, ἔρως,
the love of life, is in itself the root of all evil, and goodness lies in re-
nouncing it. Theoretically, his ethical doctrine is the extreme of so-
cialism, in a large sense; a recognition of the inner identity and equal
claims, of all men with ourselves; a recognition issuing in ἀγάπη, universal benevolence, and a stifling of particular desires.

It may come as a surprise to those who affect to hold Schopenhauer
in abhorrence, without, perhaps, really knowing the nature of his
views, that, in this theory of the essential evil of the human will—ἔρως,
the common selfish idea of life—he is reflecting and indeed probably
borrowing what he describes as the fundamental tenet of Christian theology, that *the whole creation groaneth and travaileth in pain*,[1] standing
in need of redemption. Though Schopenhauer was no friend to
Christian theology in its ordinary tendencies, he was very much in sympathy with some of the doctrines which have been connected with it.

[1]Romans viii., 22.

In his opinion the foremost truth which Christianity proclaimed to the world lay in its recognition of pessimism, its view that the world was essentially corrupt, and that the devil was its prince or ruler.[1] It would be out of place here to inquire into the exact meaning of this statement, or to determine the precise form of compensation provided for the ills of life under any scheme of doctrine which passes for Christian; and even if it were in place, the task would be an extremely difficult one; for probably no system of belief has ever undergone, at various periods, more radical changes than Christianity. But whatever prospect of happiness it may have held out, at an early date of its history, it soon came to teach that the necessary preparation for happiness, as a positive spiritual state, is *renunciation*, resignation, a looking away from external life to the inner life of the soul — *a kingdom not of this world.* So far, at least, as concerns its view of the world itself, and the main lesson and duty which life teaches, there is nothing in the theory of pessimism which does not accord with that religion which is looked up to as the guide of life over a great part of the civilised world.

What Schopenhauer does is to attempt a metaphysical explanation of the evil of life, without any reference to anything outside it. Philosophy, he urges, should be *cosmology*, not *theology*; an explanation of the world, not a scheme of divine knowledge; it should leave the gods alone — to use an ancient phrase — and claim to be left alone in return. Schopenhauer was not concerned, as the apostles and fathers of the Church were concerned, to formulate a scheme by which the ills of this life should be remedied in another — an appeal to the poor and oppressed, conveyed often in a material form, as, for instance, in the story of Dives and Lazarus. In his theory of life as the self-assertion of will, he endeavours to account for the sin, misery and iniquity of the world, and to point to the way of escape by the denial of the will to live.

Though Schopenhauer's views of life have this much in common with certain aspects of Christian doctrine, they are in decided antagonism with another theory which, though, comparatively speaking, the birth of yesterday, has already been dignified by the name of a religion, and has, no doubt, a certain number of followers. It is the theory which looks upon the life of mankind as a continual progress towards a state of perfection, and humanity in its nobler tendencies as itself worthy of worship. To those who embrace this theory, it will seem that because Schopenhauer does not hesitate to declare the evil in the life of mankind to be far in excess of the good, and as long as the human will remains what it is, any radical change for the better to be impossible, he is therefore outside the pale of civilisation, an alien from the com-

---

[1] John xii., 31.

monwealth of ordered knowledge and progress. But it has yet to be seen
how the religion of humanity will fare, either as a theory of conduct or
as a guide of life.

If there is any one doctrine more than another which has distinguished Christianity wherever it has been a living force among its adherents, it is the doctrine of renunciation; the same doctrine which, in
a different shape and with other surroundings, forms the spirit of
Buddhism. With those great religions of the world which mankind has
hitherto professed to revere as the most ennobling of all influences,
Schopenhauer's theories, not perhaps in their details, but in the principle which informs them, are, as we have seen, in close alliance.
According to him, too, renunciation, in the same sense, is the truest wisdom of life, from the higher ethical standpoint. His heroes are the
Christian ascetics of the Middle Age, and the followers of Buddha who
turn away from the Sansara to the Nirvana. But our modern habits of
thought are different. We look askance at the doctrines, and we have no
great enthusiasm for the heroes. The system which is in vogue amongst
us just now objects to the identification of nature with evil, and, in fact,
abandons ethical dualism altogether. And if nature is not evil, where, it
will be asked, is the necessity or the benefit of renunciation—a question
which may even come to be generally raised, in a not very distant future,
on behalf of some new conception of Christianity. And from another
point of view, let it be most fully and frankly admitted that renunciation
is incompatible with ordinary practice, with the rules of life as we are
compelled to formulate them; and that, to the vast majority, the doctrine
seems little but a mockery, a hopelessly unworkable plan, inapplicable
to the conditions under which men have to exist.

In spite of the fact that he is theoretically in sympathy with truths
which lie at the foundation of certain widely revered systems, the world
has not yet accepted Schopenhauer for what he proclaimed himself to
be, a great teacher; and probably for the reason that hope is not an element in his wisdom of life, and that he attenuates love into something
that is not a real, living force—a shadowy recognition of the identity of
the will. For men are disinclined to welcome a theory which neither
flatters their present position nor holds out any prospect of better things
to come. Optimism—the belief that in the end everything will be for
the best—is the natural creed of mankind; and a writer who of set purpose seeks to undermine it by an appeal to facts is regarded as one who
tries to rob humanity of its rights. How seldom an appeal to the facts
within our reach is really made! Whether the evil of life actually
outweighs the good; or, if we should look for better things, what is the
possibility or the nature of a Future Life, either for ourselves as individuals, or as part of some great whole, or, again, as contributing to a

coming state of perfection?—such inquiries claim an amount of attention which the mass of men everywhere is unwilling to give. But, in any
case, whether it is a vague assent to current beliefs, or a blind reliance
on a baseless certainty, or an impartial attempt to put away what is
false,—hope remains as the deepest foundation of every faith in a
happy future.

But it should be observed that this looking to the future as a comple-
ment for the present is dictated mainly by the desire to remedy existing
ills; and that the great hold which religion has on mankind, as an in-
centive to present happiness, is the promise it makes of coming perfection. Hope for the future is a tacit admission of evil in the present; for if
a man is completely happy in this life, and looks upon happiness as the
prevailing order, he will not think over much of another. So a discussion
of the nature of happiness is not thought complete if it takes account
only of our present life, and unless it connects what we are now and
what we do here with what we may be hereafter. Schopenhauer's theory
does not profess to do this: it promises no positive good to the individual, at most, only relief; he breaks the idol of the world, and sets up nothing in its place; and like many another iconoclast, he has long been
condemned by those whose temples he has desecrated. If there are op-
timistic theories of life, it is not life itself, he would argue, which gives
colour to them; it is rather the reflection of some great final cause which
humanity has created as the last hope of its redemption:—

> Heaven but the vision of fulfilled desire,
> And hell the shadow from a soul on fire,
>   Cast on the darkness into which ourselves,
> So late emerged from, shall so soon expire.[1]

Still, hope, it may be said, is not knowledge, nor a real answer to any
question; at most, a makeshift, a moral support for intellectual weakness. The truth is that, as theories, both optimism and pessimism are
failures, because they are extreme views where only a very partial judgment is possible. And in view of the great uncertainty of all answers,
most of those who do not accept a stereotyped system leave the question alone, as being either of little interest, or of no bearing on the welfare of their lives, which are commonly satisfied with low aims; tacitly
ridiculing those who demand an answer as the most pressing affair of
existence. But the fact that the final problems of the world are still
open, makes in favour of an honest attempt to think them out, in spite
of all previous failure or still existing difficulty; and however old these
problems may be, the endeavour to solve them is one which it is always

---

[1] Omar Khayyam; translated by E. Fitzgerald.

worth while to encourage afresh. For the individual advantages which
attend an effort to find the true path accrue quite apart from any success in reaching the goal; and even though the height we strive to climb
be inaccessible, we can still see and understand more than those who
never leave the plain. The sphere, it is true, is enormous. It is the world
and life and destiny as a whole; and our mental vision is so ill-adapted
to a range of this extent that to aim at forming a complete scheme is to
attempt the impossible. It must be recognised that the data are insufficient for large views, and that we ought not to go beyond the facts we
have, the facts of ordinary life, interpreted by the common experience
of every day. These form our only material. The views we take must of
necessity be fragmentary; they can be little but *aperçus*, rough guesses
at the undiscovered, or else of the same nature as all our possessions in
the way of knowledge—small tracts of solid land reclaimed from the
mysterious ocean of the unknown.

But if we do not admit Schopenhauer to be a great teacher, because
he is out of sympathy with the highest aspirations of mankind, and too
ready to dogmatise from partial views, he is a very suggestive writer, and
eminently readable. His style is brilliant, animated, forcible, pungent;
although it is also discursive, irresponsible, and with a tendency to superficial generalisation. He brings in the most unexpected topics without any very sure sense of their relative place; everything, in fact, seems
to be fair game, when he has taken up his pen. His irony is noteworthy;
for it extends beyond mere isolated sentences, and sometimes applies
to whole passages, which must be read *cum grano salis*. And if he has
grave faults as well as excellences of literary treatment, he is at least always witty and amusing, and that, too, in dealing with subjects—as
here, for instance, with the Conduct of Life—on which many others
have been at once severe and dull. It is easy to complain that though
he is witty and amusing, he is often at the same time bitter and ill-
natured. This is in some measure the unpleasant side of his uncom-
promising devotion to truth, his resolute eagerness to dispel illusion at
any cost—those defects of his qualities which were intensified by a soli-
tary and, until his last years, unappreciated life. He was naturally more
disposed to coerce than to flatter the world into accepting his views; he
was above all things *un esprit fort*, and at times brutal in the use of his
strength. If it should be urged that, however great his literary qualities,
he is not worth reading because he takes a narrow view of life and is
blind to some of its greatest blessings, it will be well to remember the
profound truth of that line which a friend inscribed on his earliest bi-
ography: *Si non errasset fecerat ille minus*,[1] a truth which is seldom

---

[1]Slightly altered from Martial. Epigram: I. xxii.

without application, whatever be the form of human effort. Schopenhauer cannot be neglected because he takes an unpleasant view of existence, for it is a view which must present itself, at some time, to every thoughtful person. To be outraged by Schopenhauer means to be ignorant of many of the facts of life.

In the volumes containing his *Aphorismen zur Lebensweisheit*, Schopenhauer abandons the high metaphysical standpoint, and discusses, with the same zest and appreciation as in fact marked his enjoyment of them, some of the pleasures which a wise man will seek to obtain,—health, moderate possessions, intellectual riches. And when, as in this little work, he comes to speak of the wisdom of life as the practical art of living, the pessimist view of human destiny is obtruded as little as possible. His remarks profess to be the result of a compromise— an attempt to judge life by the common standards. He is content to call these witty and instructive pages a series of aphorisms; thereby indicating that he makes no claim to expound a complete theory of conduct. It will doubtless occur to any intelligent reader that his observations are but fragmentary thoughts on various phases of life; and, in reality, mere *aphorisms*—in the old, Greek sense of the word—pithy distinctions, definitions of facts, a marking-off, as it were, of the true from the false in some of our ordinary notions of life and prosperity. Here there is little that is not in complete harmony with precepts to which the world has long been accustomed; and in this respect, also, Schopenhauer offers a suggestive comparison rather than a contrast with most writers on happiness.

The philosopher in his study is conscious that the world is never likely to embrace his higher metaphysical or ethical standpoint, and annihilate the will to live; nor did Schopenhauer himself do so except so far as, in common with most serious students of life, he avoided the ordinary aims of mankind. The theory which recommended universal benevolence as the highest ethical duty, came, in personal practice, to mean a formal standing-aloof—the *ne plus ultra* of individualism. Wisdom, as the ordinary art of living, he took to be a compromise. We are here not by any choice of our own; and while we strive to make the best of it, we must not let ourselves be deceived. If we want to be happy, he says, it will not do to cherish illusions. Schopenhauer would have found nothing admirable in the conclusion at which the late M. Edmond Scherer, for instance, arrived. *L'art de vivre,* he wrote in his preface to Amiel's *Journal, c'est de se faire une raison, de souscrire au compromis, de se prêter aux fictions.* Schopenhauer conceives his mission to be, rather, to dispel illusion, to tear the mask from life;—a violent operation, not always productive of good. Some illusion, he urges, may profitably be dispelled by recognising that no amount of external

aid will make up for inward deficiency; and that if a man has not got
the elements of happiness in himself, all the pride, pleasure, beauty
and interest of the world will not give it to him. Success in life, as
gauged by the ordinary material standard, means to place faith wholly
in externals as the source of happiness, to assert and emphasize the
common will to live, in a word, to be *vulgar*. He protests against this
search for happiness—something subjective—in the world of our surroundings, or anywhere but in a man's own self; a protest the sincerity
of which might well be imitated by some professed advocates of spiritual claims.

It would be interesting to place his utterances on this point side by
side with those of a distinguished interpreter of nature in this country,
who has recently attracted thousands of readers by describing *The
Pleasures of Life*; in other words, the blessings which the world holds
out to all who can enjoy them—health, books, friends, travel, education, art. On the common ground of their regard for these pleasures
there is no disagreement between the optimist and the pessimist. But a
characteristic difference of view may be found in the application of a
rule of life which Schopenhauer seems never to tire of repeating;
namely, that happiness consists for the most part in what a man is in
himself, and that the pleasure he derives from these blessings will depend entirely upon the extent to which his personality really allows
him to appreciate them. This is a rule which runs some risk of being
overlooked when a writer tries to dazzle the mind's eye by describing
all the possible sources of pleasure in the world of our surroundings;
but Sir John Lubbock, in common with every one who attempts a fundamental answer to the question of happiness, cannot afford to over-
look it. The truth of the rule is perhaps taken for granted in his account
of life's pleasures; but it is significant that it is only when he comes to
speak of life's troubles that he freely admits the force of it. *Happiness*,
he says, in this latter connection, *depends much more on what is within
than without us*. Yet a rigid application of this truth might perhaps dis-
count the effect of those pleasures with which the world is said to
abound. That happiness as well as unhappiness depends mainly upon
what is within, is more clearly recognised in the case of trouble; for
when troubles come upon a man. they influence him, as a rule, much
more deeply than pleasures. How few, even amongst the millions to
whom these blessings are open—health, books, travel, art—really find
any true or permanent happiness in them!

While Schopenhauer's view of the pleasures of life may be elucidated by comparing it with that of a popular writer like Sir John
Lubbock, and by contrasting the appeals they severally make to the
outer and the inner world as a source of happiness, Schopenhauer's

view of life itself will stand out more clearly if we remember the opinion so boldly expressed by the same English writer. *If we resolutely look,* observes Sir John Lubbock, *I do not say at the bright side of things, but at things as they really are; if we avail ourselves of the manifold blessings which surround us; we cannot but feel that life is indeed a glorious inheritance.*[1] There is a splendid excess of optimism about this statement which well fits it to show up the darker picture drawn by the German philosopher.

Finally, it should be remembered that though Schopenhauer's picture of the world is gloomy and sombre, there is nothing weak or unmanly in his attitude. If a happy existence, he says,—not merely an existence free from pain—is denied us, we can at least be heroes and face life with courage: *das höchste was der Mensch erlangen kann ist ein heroischer Lebenslauf.* A noble character will never complain at misfortune; for if a man looks round him at other manifestations of that which is his own inner nature, the will, he finds sorrows happening to his fellow-men harder to bear than any that have come upon himself. And the idea of nobility is to deserve the praise which Hamlet—in Shakespeare's Tragedy of Pessimism—gave to his friend:

> Thou hast been
> As one, in suffering all, that suffers nothing.

But perhaps Schopenhauer's theory carries with it its own correction. He describes existence as a more or less violent oscillation between pain and boredom. If this were really the sum of life, and we had to reason from such a partial view, it is obvious that happiness would lie in *action;* and that life would be so constituted as to supply two natural and inevitable incentives to action, and thus to contain in itself the very conditions of happiness. Life itself reveals our destiny. It is not the struggle which produces misery, it is the mistaken aims and the low ideals—*was uns alle bändigt, das Gemeine!* That life is an evil is a deduction, and possibly a mistaken deduction, from his metaphysical creed. Whether his scheme of things is correct or not—and it shares the common fate of all metaphysical systems in being unverifiable, and to that extent unprofitable—he will in the last resort have made good his claim to be read by his insight into the varied needs of human life. It may be that a future age will consign his metaphysics to the philosophical lumber-room; but he is a literary artist as well as a philosopher, and he can make a bid for fame in either capacity.

T. B. S.

DECEMBER, 1889.

---

[1] The Pleasures of Life. Part I., p. 5.

Contents

The Wisdom of Life

Le bonheur n'est pas chose aisée: il est très difficile de le trouver en nous, et impossible de le trouver ailleurs.

CHAMFORT

INTRODUCTION

IN THESE pages I shall speak of *The Wisdom of Life* in the common meaning of the term, as the art, namely, of ordering our lives so as to obtain the greatest possible amount of pleasure and success; an art the theory of which may be called *Eudæmonology*, for it teaches us how to lead a happy existence. Such an existence might perhaps be defined as one which, looked at from a purely objective point of view, or rather, after cool and mature reflection—for the question necessarily involves subjective considerations,—would be decidedly preferable to non-existence implying that we should cling to it for its own sake, and not merely from the fear of death; and further, that we should never like it to come to an end.

Now whether human life corresponds, or could possibly correspond, to this conception of existence, is a question to which, as is well-known, my philosophical system returns a negative answer. On the eudæmonistic hypothesis, however, the question must be answered in the affirmative; and I have shown, in the second volume of my chief work (ch. 49), that this hypothesis is based upon a fundamental mistake. Accordingly, in elaborating the scheme of a happy existence, I have had to make a complete surrender of the higher metaphysical and ethical standpoint to which my own theories lead; and everything I shall say here will to some extent rest upon a compromise; in so far, that is, as I take the common standpoint of every day, and embrace the error which is at the bottom of it. My remarks, therefore, will possess only a qualified value, for the very word *eudæmonology* is a euphemism. Further, I make no claims to completeness; partly because the subject is inexhaustible, and partly because I should otherwise have to say over again what has been already said by others.

The only book composed, as far as I remember, with a like purpose to that which animates this collection of aphorisms, is Cardan's *De utilitate ex adversis capienda*, which is well worth reading, and may be used to supplement the present work. Aristotle, it is true, has a few words on eudæmonology in the fifth chapter of the first book of his *Rhetoric*; but what he says does not come to very much. As compilation is not my business, I have made no use of these predecessors; more especially because in the process of compiling individuality of view is lost, and individuality of view is the kernel of works of this kind. In general, indeed, the wise in all ages have always said the same thing, and the fools, who at all times form the immense majority, have in their way, too, acted alike, and done just the opposite; and so it will continue. For, as Voltaire says, *we shall leave this world as foolish and as wicked as we found it on our arrival.*

I. DIVISION OF THE SUBJECT.

ARISTOTLE[1] divides the blessings of life into three classes—those which come to us from without, those of the soul, and those of the body. Keeping nothing of this division but the number, I observe that the fundamental differences in human lot may be reduced to three distinct classes:

(1) What a man is: that is to say, personality, in the widest sense of the word; under which are included health, strength, beauty, temperament, moral character, intelligence and education.

(2) What a man has: that is, property and possessions of every kind.

(3) How a man stands in the estimation of others: by which is to be understood, as everybody knows, what a man is in the eyes of his fellow-men, or, more strictly, the light in which they regard him. This is shown by their opinion of him; and their opinion is in its turn manifested by the honour in which he is held, and by his rank and reputation.

The differences which come under the first head are those which Nature herself has set between man and man; and from this fact alone we may at once infer that they influence the happiness or unhappiness of mankind in a much more vital and radical way than those contained under the two following heads, which are merely the effect of human arrangements. Compared with *genuine personal advantages*, such as a great mind or a great heart, all the privileges of rank or birth, even of royal birth, are but as kings on the stage to kings in real life. The same thing was said long ago by Metrodorus, the earliest disciple of Epicurus, who wrote as the title of one of his chapters, *The happiness we receive from ourselves is greater than that which we obtain from our surroundings.*[2] And it is an obvious fact, which cannot be called in question, that the principal element in a man's well-being,—indeed, in the whole tenor of his existence,—is what he is made of, his inner con-

---

[1] *Eth. Nichom.*, I. 8.
[2] Cf. Clemens Alex. Strom. II., 21.

stitution. For this is the immediate source of that inward satisfaction or dissatisfaction resulting from the sum total of his sensations, desires and thoughts; whilst his surroundings, on the other hand, exert only a mediate or indirect influence upon him. This is why the same external events or circumstances affect no two people alike; even with perfectly similar surroundings every one lives in a world of his own. For a man has immediate apprehension only of his own ideas, feelings and volitions; the outer world can influence him only in so far as it brings these to life. The world in which a man lives shapes itself chiefly by the way in which he looks at it, and so it proves different to different men; to one it is barren, dull, and superficial; to another rich, interesting, and full of meaning. On hearing of the interesting events which have happened in the course of a man's experience, many people will wish that similar things had happened in their lives too, completely forgetting that they should be envious rather of the mental aptitude which lent those events the significance they possess when he describes them. To a man of genius they were interesting adventures; but to the dull perceptions of an ordinary individual they would have been stale, everyday occurrences. This is in the highest degree the case with many of Goethe's and Byron's poems, which are obviously founded upon actual facts; where it is open to a foolish reader to envy the poet because so many delightful things happened to him, instead of envying that mighty power of phantasy which was capable of turning a fairly common experience into something so great and beautiful.

In the same way, a person of melancholy temperament will make a scene in a tragedy out of what appears to the sanguine man only in the light of an interesting conflict, and to a phlegmatic soul as something without any meaning. This all rests upon the fact that every event, in order to be realised and appreciated, requires the co-operation of two factors, namely, a subject and an object; although these are as closely and necessarily connected as oxygen and hydrogen in water. When therefore the objective or external factor in an experience is actually the same, but the subjective or personal appreciation of it varies, the event is just as much a different one in the eyes of different persons as if the objective factors had not been alike; for to a blunt intelligence the fairest and best object in the world presents only a poor reality and is therefore only poorly appreciated,—like a fine landscape in dull weather, or in the reflection of a bad *camera obscura*. In plain language, every man is pent up within the limits of his own consciousness, and cannot directly get beyond those limits any more than he can get beyond his own skin; so external aid is not of much use to him. On the stage, one man is a prince, another a minister, a third a servant or a soldier or a general, and so on,—mere external differences: the inner reality, the kernel of all these appearances is the same—a poor player, with all the anxieties of his lot. In life it is just the same. Differences of rank and wealth give every man his part to play, but this by no means implies a difference of inward happiness and pleasure; here, too, there is the same being in all—a poor mortal, with his hardships and troubles. Though these may, indeed, in every case proceed from dissimilar causes, they are in their essential nature much the same in all their forms, with degrees of intensity which vary, no doubt, but in no wise correspond to the part a man has to play, or the presence or absence of position and wealth. Since everything which exists or happens for a man exists only in his consciousness and happens for it alone, the most essential thing for a man is the constitution of this consciousness, which is in most cases far more important than the circumstances which go to form its contents. All the pride and pleasure of the world, mirrored in the dull consciousness of a fool, is poor indeed compared with the imagination of Cervantes writing his *Don Quixote* in a miserable prison. The objective half of life and reality is in the hand of fate, and accordingly takes various forms in different cases: the subjective half is ourselves, and in essentials it always remains the same.

Hence the life of every man is stamped with the same character throughout, however much his external circumstances may alter; it is like a series of variations on a single theme. No one can get beyond his own individuality. An animal, under whatever circumstances it is placed, remains within the narrow limits to which nature has irrevocably consigned it; so that our endeavours to make a pet happy must always keep within the compass of its nature, and be restricted to what it can feel. So it is with man; the measure of the happiness he can attain is determined beforehand by his individuality. More especially is this the case with the mental powers, which fix once for all his capacity for the higher kinds of pleasure. If these powers are small, no efforts from without, nothing that his fellow-men or that fortune can do for him, will suffice to raise him above the ordinary degree of human happiness and pleasure, half animal though it be. His only resources are his sensual appetite,—a cosy and cheerful family life at the most,—low company and vulgar pastime; even education, on the whole, can avail little, if anything, for the enlargement of his horizon. For the highest, most varied and lasting pleasures are those of the mind, however much our youth may deceive us on this point; and the pleasures of the mind turn chiefly on the powers of the mind. It is clear, then, that our happiness depends in a great degree upon what we *are*, upon our individuality, whilst lot or destiny is generally taken to mean only what we *have*, or our *reputation*. Our lot, in this sense, may improve; but we do not ask much of it if we are inwardly rich: on the other hand, a fool remains a fool, a dull blockhead, to his last hour, even though he were surrounded by houris in paradise. This is why Goethe, in the *West-östlicher Divan*, says that every man, whether he occupy a low position in life, or emerges as its victor, testifies to personality as the greatest factor in happiness:—

> Volk und Knecht und Ueberwinder
> Sie gestehen, zu jeder Zeit,
> Höchstes Glück der Erdenkinder
> Sei nur die Persönlichkeit.

Common experience shows that the subjective element in life is incomparably more important for our happiness and pleasure than the objective, from such sayings as *Hunger is the best sauce*, and *Youth and Age cannot live together*, up to the life of the Genius and the Saint. Health outweighs all other blessings so much that one may really say that a healthy beggar is happier than an ailing king. A quiet and cheerful temperament, happy in the enjoyment of a perfectly sound physique, an intellect clear, lively, penetrating and seeing things as they are, a moderate and gentle will, and therefore a good conscience—these are privileges which no rank or wealth can make up for or replace. For what a man is in himself, what accompanies him when he is alone, what no one can give or take away, is obviously more essential to him than everything he has in the way of possessions, or even what he may be in the eyes of the world. An intellectual man in complete solitude has excellent entertainment in his own thoughts and fancies, whilst no amount or diversity of social pleasure, theatres, excursions and amusements, can ward off boredom from a dullard. A good, temperate, gentle character can be happy in needy circumstances, whilst a covetous, envious and malicious man, even if he be the richest in the world, goes miserable. Nay more; to one who has the constant delight of a special individuality, with a high degree of intellect, most of the pleasures which are run after by mankind are perfectly superfluous; they are even a trouble and a burden. And so Horace says of himself, that, however many are deprived of the fancy-goods of life, there is one at least who can live without them:—

> Gemmas, marmor, ebur, Tyrrhena sigilla, tabellas,
> Argentum, vestes Gœtulo murice tinctas
> Sunt qui non habeant, est qui non curat habere;

and when Socrates saw various articles of luxury spread out for sale, he exclaimed: *How much there is in the world that I do not want.*

So the first and most essential element in our life's happiness is what we are,—our personality, if for no other reason than that it is a constant

factor coming into play under all circumstances. Besides, unlike the
blessings which are described under the other two heads, it is not the
sport of destiny and cannot be wrested from us; —and, so far, it is endowed with an absolute value in contrast to the merely relative worth
of the other two. The consequence of this is that it is much more difficult than people commonly suppose to get a hold on a man from without. But here the all-powerful agent, Time, comes in and claims its
rights, and before its influence physical and mental advantages gradually waste away. Moral character alone remains inaccessible to it. In
view of the destructive effect of time, it seems, indeed, as if the blessings named under the other two heads, of which time cannot directly
rob us, were superior to those of the first. Another advantage might be
claimed for them, namely, that being in their very nature objective and
external, they are attainable, and every one is presented with the possibility, at least, of coming into possession of them; whilst what is subjective is not open to us to acquire, but making its entry by a kind of *divine right*, it remains for life, immutable, inalienable, an inexorable
doom. Let me quote those lines in which Goethe describes how an unalterable destiny is assigned to every man at the hour of his birth, so that
he can develope only in the lines laid down for him, as it were, by the
conjunctions of the stars; and how the Sibyl and the prophets declare
that *himself* a man can never escape, nor any power of time avail to
change the path on which his life is cast: —

> Wie an dem Tag, der dich der Welt verliehen,
> Die Sonne stand zum Grusse der Planeten,
> Bist alsobald und fort und fort gediehen,
> Nach dem Gesetz, wonach du angetreten.
> So musst du sein, dir kannst du nicht entfliehen,
> So sagten schon Sibyllen und Propheten;
> Und keine Zeit und keine Macht zerstückelt
> Geprägte Form, die lebend sich entwickelt.

The only thing that stands in our power to achieve, is to make the
most advantageous use possible of the personal qualities we possess,
and accordingly to follow such pursuits only as will call them into play,
to strive after the kind of perfection of which they admit and to avoid
every other; consequently, to choose the position, occupation and manner of life which are most suitable for their development.

Imagine a man endowed with herculean strength who is compelled
by circumstances to follow a sedentary occupation, some minute ex-
quisite work of the hands, for example, or to engage in study and mental labour demanding quite other powers, and just those which he has
not got, —compelled, that is, to leave unused the powers in which he is

pre-eminently strong; a man placed like this will never feel happy all his life through. Even more miserable will be the lot of the man with intellectual powers of a very high order, who has to leave them undeveloped and unemployed, in the pursuit of a calling which does not require them, some bodily labour, perhaps, for which his strength is insufficient. Still, in a case of this kind, it should be our care, especially in youth, to avoid the precipice of presumption, and not ascribe to ourselves a superfluity of power which is not there.

Since the blessings described under the first head decidedly outweigh those contained under the other two, it is manifestly a wiser course to aim at the maintenance of our health and the cultivation of our faculties, than at the amassing of wealth; but this must not be mistaken as meaning that we should neglect to acquire an adequate supply of the necessaries of life. Wealth, in the strict sense of the word, that is, great superfluity, can do little for our happiness; and many rich people feel unhappy just because they are without any true mental culture or knowledge, and consequently have no objective interests which would qualify them for intellectual occupations. For beyond the satisfaction of some real and natural necessities, all that the possession of wealth can achieve has a very small influence upon our happiness, in the proper sense of the word; indeed, wealth rather disturbs it, because the preservation of property entails a great many unavoidable anxieties. And still men are a thousand times more intent on becoming rich than on acquiring culture, though it is quite certain that what a man *is* contributes much more to his happiness than what he *has*. So you may see many a man, as industrious as an ant, ceaselessly occupied from morning to night in the endeavour to increase his heap of gold. Beyond the narrow horizon of means to this end, he knows nothing; his mind is a blank, and consequently unsusceptible to any other influence. The highest pleasures, those of the intellect, are to him inaccessible, and he tries in vain to replace them by the fleeting pleasures of sense in which he indulges, lasting but a brief hour and at tremendous cost. And if he is lucky, his struggles result in his having a really great pile of gold, which he leaves to his heir, either to make it still larger, or to squander it in extravagance. A life like this, though pursued with a sense of earnestness and an air of importance, is just as silly as many another which has a fool's cap for its symbol.

What a man has in himself is, then, the chief element in his happiness. Because this is, as a rule, so very little, most of those who are placed beyond the struggle with penury, feel at bottom quite as unhappy as those who are still engaged in it. Their minds are vacant, their imagination dull, their spirits poor, and so they are driven to the company of those like them—for *similis simili gaudet*—where they make common pursuit of pastime and entertainment, consisting for the most part in sensual pleasure, amusement of every kind, and finally, in excess and libertinism. A young man of rich family enters upon life with a large patrimony, and often runs through it in an incredibly short space of time, in vicious extravagance; and why? Simply because, here too, the mind is empty and void, and so the man is bored with existence. He was sent forth into the world outwardly rich but inwardly poor, and his vain endeavour was to make his external wealth compensate for his inner poverty, by trying to obtain everything *from without*, like an old man who seeks to strengthen himself as King David or Maréchal de Retz tried to do. And so in the end one who is inwardly poor comes to be also poor outwardly.

I need not insist upon the importance of the other two kinds of blessings which make up the happiness of human life; now-a-days the value of possessing them is too well known to require advertisement. The third class, it is true, may seem, compared with the second, of a very ethereal character, as it consists only of other people's opinions. Still everyone has to strive for reputation, that is to say, a good name. Rank, on the other hand, should be aspired to only by those who serve the State, and fame by very few indeed. In any case, reputation is looked upon as a priceless treasure, and fame as the most precious of all the blessings a man can attain,—the Golden Fleece, as it were, of the elect: whilst only fools will prefer rank to property. The second and third classes, moreover, are reciprocally cause and effect; so far that is, as Petronius' maxim, *habes habeberis*, is true; and conversely, the favour of others, in all its forms, often puts us in the way of getting what we want.

II. PERSONALITY, OR WHAT A MAN IS.

WE HAVE already seen, in general, that what a man *is* contributes much more to his happiness than what he *has*, or how he is regarded by others. What a man is, and so what he has in his own person, is always the chief thing to consider; for his individuality accompanies him always and everywhere, and gives its colour to all his experiences. In every kind of enjoyment, for instance, the pleasure depends principally upon the man himself. Every one admits this in regard to physical, and how much truer it is of intellectual, pleasure. When we use that English expression, "to enjoy oneself," we are employing a very striking and appropriate phrase; for observe—one says, not "he enjoys Paris," but "he enjoys himself in Paris." To a man possessed of an ill-conditioned individuality, all pleasure is like delicate wine in a mouth made bitter with gall. Therefore, in the blessings as well as in the ills of life, less depends upon what befalls us than upon the way in which it is met, that is, upon the kind and degree of our general susceptibility. What a man is and has in himself,—in a word, personality, with all it entails, is the only immediate and direct factor in his happiness and welfare. All else is mediate and indirect, and its influence can be neutralised and frustrated; but the influence of personality never. This is why the envy which personal qualities excite is the most implacable of all,—as it is also the most carefully dissembled.

Further, the constitution of our consciousness is the ever present and lasting element in all we do or suffer; our individuality is persistently at work, more or less, at every moment of our life: all other influences are temporal, incidental, fleeting, and subject to every kind of chance and change. This is why Aristotle says: *It is not wealth but character that lasts.*[1] And just for the same reason we can more easily bear a misfortune which comes to us entirely from without, than one which we have drawn upon ourselves; for fortune may always change, but not character. Therefore, subjective blessings,—a noble nature, a capable head, a joyful temperament, bright spirits, a well-constituted, perfectly sound physique, in a word, *mens sana in corpore sano*, are the first and most important elements in happiness; so that we should be more intent on promoting and preserving such qualities than on the possession of external wealth and external honour.

And of all these, the one which makes us the most directly happy is a genial flow of good spirits; for this excellent quality is its own immediate reward. The man who is cheerful and merry has always a good reason for being so,—the fact, namely, that he is so. There is nothing which, like this quality, can so completely replace the loss of every other blessing. If you know anyone who is young, handsome, rich and esteemed, and you want to know, further, if he is happy, ask, Is he cheerful and genial?—and if he is, what does it matter whether he is young or old, straight or humpbacked, poor or rich?—he is happy. In my early days I once opened an old book and found these words: *If you laugh a great deal, you are happy; if you cry a great deal, you are unhappy;*—a very simple remark, no doubt; but just because it is so simple I have never been able to forget it, even though it is in the last degree a truism. So if cheerfulness knocks at our door, we should throw it wide open, for it never comes inopportunely. Instead of that, we often make scruples about letting it in. We want to be quite sure that we have every reason to be contented; then we are afraid that cheerfulness of spirits may interfere with serious reflections or weighty cares.

[1]Eth. Eud., vii. 2. 37:—ἡ γὰρ φύσις βέβαιον, οὐ τὰ χρήματα.

Cheerfulness is a direct and immediate gain, — the very coin, as it were, of happiness, and not, like all else, merely a cheque upon the bank; for it alone makes us immediately happy in the present moment, and that is the highest blessing for beings like us, whose existence is but an infinitesimal moment between two eternities. To secure and promote this feeling of cheerfulness should be the supreme aim of all our endeavours after happiness.

Now it is certain that nothing contributes so little to cheerfulness as riches, or so much, as health. Is it not in the lower classes, the so-called working classes, more especially those of them who live in the country, that we see cheerful and contented faces? and is it not amongst the rich, the upper classes, that we find faces full of ill-humour and vexation? Consequently we should try as much as possible to maintain a high degree of health; for cheerfulness is the very flower of it. I need hardly say what one must do to be healthy — avoid every kind of excess, all violent and unpleasant emotion, all mental overstrain, take daily exercise in the open air, cold baths and such like hygienic measures. For without a proper amount of daily exercise no one can remain healthy; all the processes of life demand exercise for the due performance of their functions, exercise not only of the parts more immediately concerned, but also of the whole body. For, as Aristotle rightly says, *Life is movement;* it is its very essence. Ceaseless and rapid motion goes on in every part of the organism. The heart, with its complicated double systole and diastole, beats strongly and untiringly; with twenty-eight beats it has to drive the whole of the blood through arteries, veins and capillaries; the lungs pump like a steam-engine, without intermission; the intestines are always in peristaltic action; the glands are all constantly absorbing and secreting; even the brain has a double motion of its own, with every beat of the pulse and every breath we draw. When people can get no exercise at all, as is the case with the countless numbers who are condemned to a sedentary life, there is a glaring and fatal disproportion between outward inactivity and inner tumult. For this ceaseless internal motion requires some external counterpart, and the want of it produces effects like those of emotion which we are obliged to suppress. Even trees must be shaken by the wind, if they are to thrive. The rule which finds its application here may be most briefly expressed in Latin: *omnis motus, quo celerior, eo magis motus.*

How much our happiness depends upon our spirits, and these again upon our state of health, may be seen by comparing the influence which the same external circumstances or events have upon us when we are well and strong with the effect which they have when we are depressed and troubled with ill-health. It is not what things are objectively and in themselves, but what they are for us, in our way of looking at them, that makes us happy or the reverse. As Epictetus says, *Men are not influenced by things but by their thoughts about things.* And, in general, nine-tenths of our happiness depends upon health alone. With health, everything is a source of pleasure; without it, nothing else, whatever it may be, is enjoyable; even the other personal blessings,—a great mind, a happy temperament—are degraded and dwarfed for want of it. So it is really with good reason that, when two people meet, the first thing they do is to inquire after each other's health, and to express the hope that it is good; for good health is by far the most important element in human happiness. It follows from all this that the greatest of follies is to sacrifice health for any other kind of happiness, whatever it may be, for gain, advancement, learning or fame, let alone, then, for fleeting sensual pleasures. Everything else should rather be postponed to it.

But however much health may contribute to that flow of good spirits which is so essential to our happiness, good spirits do not entirely depend upon health; for a man may be perfectly sound in his physique and still possess a melancholy temperament and be generally given up to sad thoughts. The ultimate cause of this is undoubtedly to be found in innate, and therefore unalterable, physical constitution, especially in the more or less normal relation of a man's sensitiveness to his muscular and vital energy. Abnormal sensitiveness produces inequality of spirits, a predominating melancholy, with periodical fits of unrestrained liveliness. A genius is one whose nervous power or sensitiveness is largely in excess; as Aristotle[1] has very correctly observed, *Men distinguished in philosophy, politics, poetry or art, appear to be all of a melancholy temperament.* This is doubtless the passage which Cicero has in his mind when he says, as he often does, *Aristoteles ait omnes ingeniosos melancholicos esse.*[2] Shakespeare has very neatly expressed this radical and innate diversity of temperament in those lines in *The Merchant of Venice:*

> Nature has framed strange fellows in her time;
> Some that will evermore peep through their eyes,
> And laugh, like parrots at a bag-piper;
> And others of such vinegar aspect,
> That they'll not show their teeth in way of smile,
> Though Nestor swear the jest be laughable.

This is the difference which Plato draws between εὔκολος and δύσκολος—the man of *easy*, and the man of *difficult* disposition—in proof of which he refers to the varying degrees of susceptibility which

---

[1] *Probl.* xxx, ep. 1.
[2] *Tusc.* i., 33.

different people show to pleasurable and painful impressions; so that one man will laugh at what makes another despair. As a rule, the stronger the susceptibility to unpleasant impressions, the weaker is the susceptibility to pleasant ones, and *vice versa*. If it is equally possible for an event to turn out well or ill, the δύσκολος will be annoyed or grieved if the issue is unfavourable, and will not rejoice, should it be happy. On the other hand, the εὔκολος will neither worry nor fret over an unfavourable issue, but rejoice if it turns out well. If the one is successful in nine out of ten undertakings, he will not be pleased, but rather annoyed that one has miscarried; whilst the other, if only a single one succeeds, will manage to find consolation in the fact and remain cheerful. But here is another instance of the truth, that hardly any evil is entirely without its compensation; for the misfortunes and sufferings which the δύσκολοι, that is, people of gloomy and anxious character, have to overcome, are, on the whole, more imaginary and therefore less real than those which befall the gay and careless; for a man who paints everything black, who constantly fears the worst and takes measures accordingly, will not be disappointed so often in this world, as one who always looks upon the bright side of things. And when a morbid affection of the nerves, or a derangement of the digestive organs, plays into the hand of an innate tendency to gloom, this tendency may reach such a height that permanent discomfort produces a weariness of life. So arises an inclination to suicide, which even the most trivial unpleasantness may actually bring about; nay, when the tendency attains its worst form, it may be occasioned by nothing in particular, but a man may resolve to put an end to his existence, simply because he is permanently unhappy, and then coolly and firmly carry out his determination; as may be seen by the way in which the sufferer, when placed under supervision, as he usually is, eagerly waits to seize the first unguarded moment, when, without a shudder, without a struggle or recoil, he may use the now natural and welcome means of effecting his release.[1] Even the healthiest, perhaps even the most cheerful man, may resolve upon death under certain circumstances; when, for instance, his sufferings, or his fears of some inevitable misfortune, reach such a pitch as to outweigh the terrors of death. The only difference lies in the degree of suffering necessary to bring about the fatal act, a degree which will be high in the case of a cheerful, and low in that of a gloomy man. The greater the melancholy, the lower need the degree be; in the end, it may even sink to zero. But if a man is cheerful, and his spirits are supported by good health, it requires a high degree of suffering to make him lay hands upon himself. There are

---

[1] For a detailed description of this condition of mind *cf.* Esquirol *Des maladies mentales*.

countless steps in the scale between the two extremes of suicide, the suicide which springs merely from a morbid intensification of innate gloom, and the suicide of the healthy and cheerful man, who has entirely objective grounds for putting an end to his existence.

Beauty is partly an affair of health. It may be reckoned as a personal advantage; though it does not, properly speaking, contribute directly to our happiness. It does so indirectly, by impressing other people; and it is no unimportant advantage, even in man. Beauty is an open letter of recommendation, predisposing the heart to favour the person who presents it. As is well said in those lines of Homer, the gift of beauty is not lightly to be thrown away, that glorious gift which none can bestow save the gods alone—

οὔτοι ἀπόβλητ᾽ ἐστὶ θεῶν ἐρικυδέα δῶρα,
ὅσσα κεν αὐτοὶ δῶσιν, ἑκὼν δ᾽οὐκ ἄν τις ἕλοιτο.[1]

The most general survey shows us that the two foes of human happiness are pain and boredom. We may go further, and say that in the degree in which we are fortunate enough to get away from the one, we approach the other. Life presents, in fact, a more or less violent oscillation between the two. The reason of this is that each of these two poles stands in a double antagonism to the other, external or objective, and inner or subjective. Needy surroundings and poverty produce pain; while, if a man is more than well off, he is bored. Accordingly, while the lower classes are engaged in a ceaseless struggle with need, in other words, with pain, the upper carry on a constant and often desperate battle with boredom.[2] The inner or subjective antagonism arises from the fact that, in the individual, susceptibility to pain varies inversely with susceptibility to boredom, because susceptibility is directly proportionate to mental power. Let me explain. A dull mind is, as a rule associated with dull sensibilities, nerves which no stimulus can affect, a temperament, in short, which does not feel pain or anxiety very much, however great or terrible it may be. Now, intellectual dullness is at the bottom of that *vacuity of soul* which is stamped on so many faces, a state of mind which betrays itself by a constant and lively attention to all the trivial circumstances in the external world. This is the true source of boredom—a continual panting after excitement, in order to have a pretext for giving the mind and spirits something to occupy them. The kind of things people choose for this purpose shows that they are not very particular, as witness the miserable pastimes they have

---

[1] *Iliad* 3, 65.
[2] And the extremes meet; for the lowest state of civilization, a nomad or wandering life, finds its counterpart in the highest, where everyone is at times a tourist. The earlier stage was a case of necessity; the latter is a remedy for boredom.

recourse to, and their ideas of social pleasure and conversation; or again, the number of people who gossip on the doorstep or gape out of the window. It is mainly because of this inner vacuity of soul that people go in quest of society, diversion, amusement, luxury of every sort, which lead many to extravagance and misery. Nothing is so good a protection against such misery as inward wealth, the wealth of the mind, because the greater it grows, the less room it leaves for boredom. The inexhaustible activity of thought! finding ever new material to work upon in the multifarious phenomena of self and nature, and able and ready to form new combinations of them,—there you have something that invigorates the mind, and apart from moments of relaxation, sets it far above the reach of boredom.

But, on the other hand, this high degree of intelligence is rooted in a high degree of susceptibility, greater strength of will, greater passionateness; and from the union of these qualities comes an increased capacity for emotion, an enhanced sensibility to all mental and even bodily pain, greater impatience of obstacles, greater resentment of interruption;—all of which tendencies are augmented by the power of the imagination, the vivid character of the whole range of thought, including what is disagreeable. This applies, in varying degrees, to every step in the long scale of mental power, from the veriest dunce to the greatest genius that ever lived. Therefore the nearer anyone is, either from a subjective or from an objective point of view, to one of these sources of suffering in human life, the farther he is from the other. And so a man's natural bent will lead him to make his objective world conform to his subjective as much as possible; that is to say, he will take the greatest measures against that form of suffering to which he is most liable. The wise man will, above all, strive after freedom from pain and annoyance, quiet and leisure, consequently a tranquil, modest life, with as few encounters as may be; and so, after a little experience of his so-called fellow-men, he will elect to live in retirement, or even, if he is a man of great intellect, in solitude. For the more a man has in himself, the less he will want from other people,—the less, indeed, other people can be to him. This is why a high degree of intellect tends to make a man unsocial. True, if *quality* of intellect could be made up for by *quantity*, it might be worth while to live even in the great world; but, unfortunately, a hundred fools together will not make one wise man.

But the individual who stands at the other end of the scale is no sooner free from the pangs of need than he endeavours to get pastime and society at any cost, taking up with the first person he meets, and avoiding nothing so much as himself. For in solitude, where every one is thrown upon his own resources, what a man has in himself comes to light: the fool in fine raiment groans under the burden of his miserable personality, a burden which he can never throw off, whilst the man of talent peoples the waste places with his animating thoughts. Seneca declares that folly is its own burden, — *omnis stultitia laborat fastidio sui*, — a very true saying, with which may be compared the words of Jesus, the son of Sirach, *The life of a fool is worse than death*.[1] And, as a rule, it will be found that a man is sociable just in the degree in which he is intellectually poor and generally vulgar. For one's choice in this world does not go much beyond solitude on one side and vulgarity on the other. It is said that the most sociable of all people are the Negroes and they are at the bottom of the scale in intellect. I remember reading once in a French paper[2] that the blacks in North America, whether free or enslaved, are fond of shutting themselves up in large numbers in the smallest space, because they cannot have too much of one another's snub-nosed company.

The brain may be regarded as a kind of parasite of the organism, a pensioner, as it were, who dwells with the body: and leisure, that is, the time one has for the free enjoyment of one's consciousness or individuality, is the fruit or produce of the rest of existence, which is in general only labour and effort. But what does most people's leisure yield? — boredom and dullness; except, of course, when it is occupied with sensual pleasure or folly. How little such leisure is worth may be seen in the way in which it is spent: and, as Ariosto observes, how miserable are the idle hours of ignorant men! — *ozio lungo d'uomini ignoranti*. Ordinary people think merely how they shall *spend* their time; a man of any talent tries to *use* it. The reason why people of limited intellect are apt to be bored is that their intellect is absolutely nothing more than the means by which the motive power of the will is put into force; and whenever there is nothing particular to set the will in motion, it rests, and their intellect takes a holiday, because, equally with the will, it requires something external to bring it into play. The result is an awful stagnation of whatever power a man has — in a word, boredom. To counteract this miserable feeling, men run to trivialities which please for the moment they are taken up, hoping thus to engage the will in order to rouse it to action, and so set the intellect in motion; for it is the latter which has to give effect to these motives of the will. Compared with real and natural motives, these are but as paper money to coin; for their value is only arbitrary — card games and the like, which have been invented for this very purpose. And if there is nothing else to be done, a man will twirl his thumbs or beat the devil's tattoo; or a cigar may be a welcome substitute for exercising his brains. Hence,

---

[1] Ecclesiasticus, xxii. 11.
[2] *Le Commerce*, Oct. 19th, 1837.

in all countries the chief occupation of society is card-playing,[1] and it is the gauge of its value, and an outward sign that it is bankrupt in thought. Because people have no thoughts to deal in, they deal cards, and try and win one another's money. Idiots! But I do not wish to be unjust; so let me remark that it may certainly be said in defence of card-playing that it is a preparation for the world and for business life, because one learns thereby how to make a clever use of fortuitous but unalterable circumstances, (cards, in this case), and to get as much out of them as one can: and to do this a man must learn a little dissimulation, and how to put a good face upon a bad business. But, on the other hand, it is exactly for this reason that card-playing is so demoralising, since the whole object of it is to employ every kind of trick and machination in order to win what belongs to another. And a habit of this sort, learnt at the card-table, strikes root and pushes its way into practical life; and in the affairs of every day a man gradually comes to regard *meum* and *tuum* in much the same light as cards, and to consider that he may use to the utmost whatever advantages he possesses, so long as he does not come within the arm of the law. Examples of what I mean are of daily occurrence in mercantile life. Since, then, leisure is the flower, or rather the fruit, of existence, as it puts a man into possession of himself, those are happy indeed who possess something real in themselves. But what do you get from most people's leisure?—only a good-for-nothing fellow, who is terribly bored and a burden to himself. Let us, therefore, rejoice, dear brethren, for *we are not children of the bondwoman, but of the free.*

Further, as no land is so well off as that which requires few imports, or none at all, so the happiest man is one who has enough in his own inner wealth, and asks little or nothing from outside for his maintenance. For imports are expensive things, reveal dependence, entail danger, occasion trouble, and, when all is said and done, are a poor substitute for home produce. No man ought to expect much from others, or, in general, from the external world. What one human being can be to another is not a very great deal: in the end every one stands alone, and the important thing is *who* it is that stands alone. Here, then, is another application of the general truth which Goethe recognises in *Dichtung und Wahrheit* (Bk. III.), that in everything a man has ultimately to appeal to himself; or, as Goldsmith puts it in *The Traveller*:

> Still to ourselves in every place consign'd
> Our own felicity we make or find.

---

[1] *Translator's Note.*—Card-playing to this extent is now, no doubt, a thing of the past, at any rate amongst the nations of northern Europe. The present fashion is rather in favour of a dilettante interest in art or literature.

Himself is the source of the best and most a man can be or achieve. The more this is so—the more a man finds his sources of pleasure in himself—the happier he will be. Therefore, it is with great truth that Aristotle[1] says, *To be happy means to be self-sufficient.* For all other sources of happiness are in their nature most uncertain, precarious, fleeting, the sport of chance; and so even under the most favourable circumstances they can easily be exhausted; nay, this is unavoidable, because they are not always within reach. And in old age these sources of happiness most necessarily dry up:—love leaves us then, and wit, desire to travel, delight in horses, aptitude for social intercourse; friends and relations, too, are taken from us by death. Then more than ever, it depends upon what a man has in himself; for this will stick to him longest; and at any period of life it is the only genuine and lasting source of happiness. There is not much to be got anywhere in the world. It is filled with misery and pain; and if a man escapes these, boredom lies in wait for him at every corner. Nay more; it is evil which generally has the upper hand, and folly makes the most noise. Fate is cruel, and mankind pitiable. In such a world as this, a man who is rich in himself is like a bright, warm, happy room at Christmastide, while without are the frost and snow of a December night. Therefore, without doubt, the happiest destiny on earth is to have the rare gift of a rich individuality, and, more especially, to be possessed of a good endowment of intellect; this is the happiest destiny, though it may not be, after all, a very brilliant one. There was great wisdom in that remark which Queen Christina of Sweden made, in her nineteenth year, about Descartes, who had then lived for twenty years in the deepest solitude in Holland, and, apart from report, was known to her only by a single essay: *M. Descartes,* she said, *is the happiest of men, and his condition seems to me much to be envied.*[2] Of course, as was the case with Descartes, external circumstances must be favourable enough to allow a man to be master of his life and happiness; or, as we read in *Ecclesiastes,*[3]—*Wisdom is good together with an inheritance, and profitable unto them that see the sun.* The man to whom nature and fate have granted the blessing of wisdom, will be most anxious and careful to keep open the fountains of happiness which he has in himself; and for this, independence and leisure are necessary. To obtain them, he will be willing to moderate his desires and harbour his resources; all the more because he is not, like others, restricted to the external world for his pleasures. So he will not be misled by expectations of office, or

---

[1] Eth. Eud., vii. 2.
[2] *Vie de Descartes*, par Baillet. Liv. vii., ch. 10.
[3] vii. 12.

money, or the favour and applause of his fellow-men, into surrendering himself in order to conform to low desires and vulgar tastes; nay, in such a case he will follow the advice that Horace gives in his epistle to Mæcenas.[1] It is a great piece of folly to sacrifice the inner for the outer man, to give the whole or the greater part of one's quiet leisure and independence for splendour, rank, pomp, titles and honour. This is what Goethe did. My good luck drew me quite in the other direction.

The truth which I am insisting upon here, the truth, namely, that the chief source of human happiness is internal, is confirmed by that most accurate observation of Aristotle in the *Nichomachean Ethics*,[2] that every pleasure presupposes some sort of activity, the application of some sort of power, without which it cannot exist. The doctrine of Aristotle's, that a man's happiness consists in the free exercise of his highest faculties, is also enunciated by Stobæus in his exposition of the Peripatetic philosophy:[3] *Happiness*, he says, *means vigorous and successful activity in all your undertakings*; and he explains that by *vigour* (ἀρέτη) he means *mastery* in any thing, whatever it be. Now, the original purpose of those forces with which nature has endowed man is to enable him to struggle against the difficulties which beset him on all sides. But if this struggle comes to an end, his unemployed forces become a burden to him; and he has to set to work and play with them,— use them, I mean, for no purpose at all, beyond avoiding the other source of human suffering, boredom, to which he is at once exposed. It is the upper classes, people of wealth, who are the greatest victims of boredom. Lucretius long ago described their miserable state, and the truth of his description may be still recognised to-day in the life of every great capital—where the rich man is seldom in his own halls, because it bores him to be there, and still he returns thither, because he is no better off outside;—or else he is away in posthaste to his house in the country, as if it were on fire and he is no sooner arrived there, than he is bored again, and seeks to forget everything in sleep, or else hurries back to town once more.

> Exit saepe foras magnis ex œdibus ille,
> Esse domi quem pertaesum est, subitoque reventat;
> Quippe foris nihilo melius qui sentiat esse.
> Currit, agens mannos, ad villam precipitanter,
> Auxilium tectis quasi ferre ardentibus instans:
> Oscitat extemplo, tetigit quum limina villae;

---

[1]Lib. 1., ep. 7.

   Nec somnum plebis laudo, satur altilium, nec
   Otia divitiis Arabum liberrima muto.

[2]i. 7 and vii, 13, 14.

[3]Ecl. eth. ii., ch. 7.

Aut abit in somnum gravis, atque oblivia quaerit;
Aut etiam properans urbem petit atque revisit.[1]

In their youth, such people must have had a superfluity of muscular
and vital energy,—powers which, unlike those of the mind, cannot
maintain their full degree of vigour very long; and in later years they either have no mental powers at all, or cannot develope any for want of
employment which would bring them into play; so that they are in a
wretched plight. *Will*, however, they still possess, for this is the only
power that is inexhaustible; and they try to stimulate their will by passionate excitement, such as games of chance for high stakes—undoubtedly a most degrading form of vice. And one may say generally
that if a man finds himself with nothing to do, he is sure to choose
some amusement suited to the kind of power in which he excels,—
bowls, it may be, or chess; hunting or painting; horse-racing or music;
cards, or poetry, heraldry, philosophy, or some other dilettante interest.
We might classify these interests methodically, by reducing them to ex-
pressions of the three fundamental powers, the factors, that is to say,
which go to make up the physiological constitution of man; and further, by considering these powers by themselves, and apart from any of
the definite aims which they may subserve, and simply as affording
three sources of possible pleasure, out of which every man will choose
what suits him, according as he excels in one direction or another.

First of all come the pleasures of *vital energy*, of food, drink, diges-
tion, rest and sleep; and there are parts of the world where it can be said
that these are characteristic and national pleasures. Secondly, there are
the pleasures of *muscular energy*, such as walking, running, wrestling,
dancing, fencing, riding and similar athletic pursuits, which sometimes
take the form of sport, and sometimes of a military life and real warfare.
Thirdly, there are the pleasures of *sensibility*, such as observation,
thought, feeling, or a taste for poetry or culture, music, learning, reading, meditation, invention, philosophy and the like. As regards the
value, relative worth and duration of each of these kinds of pleasure, a
great deal might be said, which, however, I leave the reader to supply.
But every one will see that the nobler the power which is brought into
play, the greater will be the pleasure which it gives; for pleasure always
involves the use of one's own powers, and happiness consists in a frequent repetition of pleasure. No one will deny that in this respect the
pleasures of sensibility occupy a higher place than either of the other
two fundamental kinds; which exist in an equal, nay, in a greater degree in brutes; it is his preponderating amount of sensibility which dis-
tinguishes man from other animals. Now, our mental powers are forms

[1]III. 1079.

of sensibility, and therefore a preponderating amount of it makes us capable of that kind of pleasure which has to do with mind, so-called intellectual pleasure; and the more sensibility predominates, the greater the pleasure will be.[1]

The normal, ordinary man takes a vivid interest in anything only in so far as it excites his will, that is to say, is a matter of personal interest to him. But constant excitement of the will is never an unmixed good, to say the least; in other words, it involves pain. Card-playing, that universal occupation of "good society" everywhere, is a device for providing this kind of excitement, and that, too, by means of interests so small as to produce slight and momentary, instead of real and permanent, pain. Card-playing is, in fact, a mere tickling of the will.[2]

---

[1]Nature exhibits a continual progress, starting from the mechanical and chemical activity of the inorganic world, proceeding to the vegetable, with its dull enjoyment of self, from that to the animal world, where intelligence and consciousness begin, at first very weak, and only after many intermediate stages attaining its last great development in man, whose intellect is Nature's crowning point, the goal of all her efforts, the most perfect and difficult of all her works. And even within the range of the human intellect, there are a great many observable differences of degree, and it is very seldom that intellect reaches its highest point, intelligence properly so-called, which in this narrow and strict sense of the word, is Nature's most consummate product, and so the rarest and most precious thing of which the world can boast. The highest product of Nature is the clearest degree of consciousness, in which the world mirrors itself more plainly and completely than anywhere else. A man endowed with this form of intelligence is in possession of what is noblest and best on earth; and accordingly, he has a source of pleasure in comparison with which all others are small. From his surroundings he asks nothing but leisure for the free enjoyment of what he has got, time, as it were, to polish his diamond. All other pleasures that are not of the intellect are of a lower kind; for they are, one and all, movements of will—desires, hopes, fears and ambitions, no matter to what directed: they are always satisfied at the cost of pain, and in the case of ambition, generally with more or less of illusion. With intellectual pleasure, on the other hand, truth becomes clearer and clearer. In the realm of intelligence pain has no power. Knowledge is all in all. Further, intellectual pleasures are accessible entirely and only through the medium of the intelligence, and are limited by its capacity. *For all the wit there is in the world is useless to him who has none.* Still this advantage is accompanied by a substantial disadvantage; for the whole of Nature shows that with the growth of intelligence comes increased capacity for pain, and it is only with the highest degree of intelligence that suffering reaches its supreme point.

[2]*Vulgarity* is, at bottom, the kind of consciousness in which the will completely predominates over the intellect, where the latter does nothing more than perform the service of its master, the will. Therefore, when the will makes no demands, supplies no motives, strong or weak, the intellect entirely loses its power, and the result is complete vacancy of mind. Now *will without intellect* is the most vulgar and common thing in the world, possessed by every blockhead, who, in the gratification of his passions, shows the stuff of which he is made. This is the condition of mind called *vulgarity*, in which the only active elements are the organs of sense, and that small amount of intellect which is necessary for apprehending the data of sense. Accordingly, the vulgar man is constantly open to all sorts of impressions, and immediately perceives all the little

On the other hand, a man of powerful intellect is capable of taking a vivid interest in things in the way of mere *knowledge*, with no admixture of *will*; nay, such an interest is a necessity to him. It places him in a sphere where pain is an alien, a diviner air where the gods live serene: —

θεοὶ ῥεῖα ζώοντες.[1]

Look on these two pictures—the life of the masses, one long, dull record of struggle and effort entirely devoted to the petty interests of personal welfare, to misery in all its forms, a life beset by intolerable boredom as soon as ever those aims are satisfied and the man is thrown back upon himself, whence he can be roused again to some sort of movement only by the wild fire of passion. On the other side you have a man endowed with a high degree of mental power, leading an existence rich in thought and full of life and meaning, occupied by worthy and interesting objects as soon as ever he is free to give himself to them, bearing in himself a source of the noblest pleasure. What external promptings he wants come from the works of nature, and from the contemplation of human affairs and the achievements of the great of all ages and countries, which are thoroughly appreciated by a man of this type alone, as being the only one who can quite understand and feel with them. And so it is for him alone that those great ones have really lived; it is to him that they make their appeal; the rest are but casual hearers, who only half understand either them or their followers. Of course, this characteristic of the intellectual man implies that he has one more need than the others, the need of reading, observing, studying, meditating, practising, the need, in short, of undisturbed leisure. For, as Voltaire has very rightly said, *there are no real pleasures without real needs*; and the need of them is why to such a man pleasures are accessible which are denied to others,—the varied beauties of nature and art and literature. To heap these round people who do not want them and cannot appreciate them, is like expecting grey hairs to fall in love. A man who is privileged in this respect leads two lives, a personal and an intellectual, life; and the latter gradually comes to be looked upon as the true one, and the former as merely a means to it. Other people make this shallow, empty and troubled existence an end in itself. To the life of the intellect such a man will give the preference over all his

---

trifling things that go on in his environment: the lightest whisper, the most trivial circumstance, is sufficient to rouse his attention; he is just like an animal. Such a man's mental condition reveals itself in his face, in his whole exterior; and hence that vulgar, repulsive appearance, which is all the more offensive, if, as is usually the case, his will—the only factor in his consciousness—is a base, selfish and altogether bad one.

[1] *Odyssey* IV., 805.

other occupations: by the constant growth of insight and knowledge, this intellectual life, like a slowly-forming work of art, will acquire a consistency, a permanent intensity, a unity which becomes ever more and more complete; compared with which, a life devoted to the attainment of personal comfort, a life that may broaden indeed, but can never be deepened, makes but a poor show: and yet, as I have said, people make this baser sort of existence an end in itself.

The ordinary life of every day, so far as it is not moved by passion, is tedious and insipid; and if it is so moved, it soon becomes painful. Those alone are happy whom nature has favoured with some superfluity of intellect, something beyond what is just necessary to carry out the behests of their will; for it enables them to lead an intellectual life as well, a life unattended by pain and full of vivid interests. Mere leisure, that is to say, intellect unoccupied in the service of the will, is not of itself sufficient: there must be a real superfluity of power, set free from the service of the will and devoted to that of the intellect; for, as Seneca says, *otium sine litteris mors est et vivi hominis sepultura* — illiterate leisure is a form of death, a living tomb. Varying with the amount of the superfluity, there will be countless developments in this second life, the life of the mind; it may be the mere collection and labelling of insects, birds, minerals, coins, or the highest achievements of poetry and philosophy. The life of the mind is not only a protection against boredom, it also wards off the pernicious effects of boredom; it keeps us from bad company, from the many dangers, misfortunes, losses and extravagances which the man who places his happiness entirely in the objective world is sure to encounter. My philosophy, for instance, has never brought me in a sixpence; but it has spared me many an expense.

The ordinary man places his life's happiness in things external to him, in property, rank, wife and children, friends, society, and the like, so that when he loses them or finds them disappointing, the foundation of his happiness is destroyed. In other words, his centre of gravity is not in himself; it is constantly changing its place, with every wish and whim. If he is a man of means, one day it will be his house in the country, another buying horses, or entertaining friends, or travelling, — a life, in short, of general luxury, the reason being that he seeks his pleasure in things outside him. Like one whose health and strength are gone, he tries to regain by the use of jellies and drugs, instead of by developing his own vital power, the true source of what he has lost. Before proceeding to the opposite, let us compare with this common type the man who comes midway between the two, endowed, it may be, not exactly with distinguished powers of mind, but with somewhat more than the ordinary amount of intellect. He will take a dilettante interest in art, or devote his attention to some branch of science — botany, for example, or physics, astronomy, history, and find a great deal of pleasure in such studies, and amuse himself with them when external sources of happiness are exhausted or fail to satisfy him any more. Of a man like this it may be said that his centre of gravity is partly in himself. But a dilettante interest in art is a very different thing from creative activity; and an amateur pursuit of science is apt to be superficial and not to penetrate to the heart of the matter. A man cannot entirely identify himself with such pursuits, or have his whole existence so completely filled and permeated with them that he loses all interest in everything else. It is only the highest intellectual power, what we call *genius*, that attains to this degree of intensity, making all time and existence its theme, and striving to express its peculiar conception of the world, whether it contemplates life as the subject of poetry or of philosophy. Hence, undisturbed occupation with himself, his own thoughts and works, is a matter of urgent necessity to such a man; solitude is welcome, leisure is the highest good, and everything else is unnecessary, nay, even burdensome.

This is the only type of man of whom it can be said that his centre of gravity is entirely in himself; which explains why it is that people of this sort—and they are very rare—no matter how excellent their character may be, do not show that warm and unlimited interest in friends, family, and the community in general, of which others are so often capable; for if they have only themselves they are not inconsolable for the loss of everything else. This gives an isolation to their character, which is all the more effective since other people never really quite satisfy them, as being, on the whole, of a different nature: nay more, since this difference is constantly forcing itself upon their notice, they get accustomed to move about amongst mankind as alien beings, and in thinking of humanity in general, to say *they* instead of *we*.

So the conclusion we come to is that the man whom nature has endowed with intellectual wealth is the happiest; so true it is that the subjective concerns us more than the objective; for whatever the latter may be, it can work only indirectly, secondarily, and through the medium of the former—a truth finely expressed by Lucian:—

Πλοῦτος ὁ τῆς ψυχῆς πλοῦτος μόνος ἐστὶν ἀληθής
Τἆλλα δ᾽ ἔχει ἄτην πλείονα τῶν κτεάνων[1]

—the wealth of the soul is the only true wealth, for with all other riches comes a bane even greater than they. The man of inner wealth wants nothing from outside but the negative gift of undisturbed leisure, to develop and mature his intellectual faculties, that is, to enjoy his wealth;

[1]Epigrammata, 12.

in short, he wants permission to be himself, his whole life long, every day and every hour. If he is destined to impress the character of his mind upon a whole race, he has only one measure of happiness or un-happiness—to succeed or fail in perfecting his powers and completing his work. All else is of small consequence. Accordingly, the greatest minds of all ages have set the highest value upon undisturbed leisure, as worth exactly as much as the man himself. *Happiness appears to con-sist in leisure,* says Aristotle;[1] and Diogenes Laertius reports that *Socrates praised leisure as the fairest of all possessions.* So, in the *Nichomachean Ethics,* Aristotle concludes that a life devoted to philos-ophy is the happiest; or, as he says in the *Politics,*[2] *the free exercise of any power, whatever it may be, is happiness.* This, again, tallies with what Goethe says in *Wilhelm Meister: The man who is born with a tal-ent which he is meant to use, finds his greatest happiness in using it.*

But to be in possession of undisturbed leisure is far from being the common lot; nay, it is something alien to human nature, for the ordi-nary man's destiny is to spend life in procuring what is necessary for the subsistence of himself and his family; he is a son of struggle and need, not a free intelligence. So people as a rule soon get tired of undisturbed leisure, and it becomes burdensome if there are no fictitious and forced aims to occupy it, play, pastime and hobbies of every kind. For this very reason it is full of possible danger, and *difficilis in otio quies* is a true saying,—it is difficult to keep quiet if you have nothing to do. On the other hand, a measure of intellect far surpassing the ordinary is as un-natural as it is abnormal. But if it exists, and the man endowed with it is to be happy, he will want precisely that undisturbed leisure which the others find burdensome or pernicious; for without it he is a Pegasus in harness, and consequently unhappy. If these two unnatural circum-stances, external and internal, undisturbed leisure and great intellect, happen to coincide in the same person, it is a great piece of fortune; and if fate is so far favourable, a man can lead the higher life, the life protected from the two opposite sources of human suffering, pain and boredom, from the painful struggle for existence, and the incapacity for enduring leisure (which is free existence itself)—evils which may be es-caped only by being mutually neutralised.

But there is something to be said in opposition to this view. Great in-tellectual gifts mean an activity pre-eminently nervous in its character, and consequently a very high degree of susceptibility to pain in every form. Further, such gifts imply an intense temperament, larger and more vivid ideas, which, as the inseparable accompaniment of great in-

---

[1]Eth. Nichom. x. 7.
[2]iv. 11.

tellectual power, entail on its possessor a corresponding intensity of the
emotions, making them incomparably more violent than those to
which the ordinary man is a prey. Now, there are more things in the
world productive of pain than of pleasure. Again, a large endowment of
intellect tends to estrange the man who has it from other people and
their doings; for the more a man has in himself, the less he will be able
to find in them; and the hundred things in which they take delight, he
will think shallow and insipid. Here, then, perhaps, is another instance
of that law of compensation which makes itself felt everywhere. How
often one hears it said, and said, too, with some plausibility, that the
narrow-minded man is at bottom the happiest, even though his fortune
is unenviable. I shall make no attempt to forestall the reader's own
judgment on this point; more especially as Sophocles himself has given
utterance to two diametrically opposite opinions:—

Πολλῷ τὸ φρονεῖν εὐδαιμονίας
πρῶτον ὑπάρχει.[1]

he says in one place—wisdom is the greatest part of happiness; and
again, in another passage, he declares that the life of the thoughtless is
the most pleasant of all—

Ἐν τῷ φρονεῖν γὰρ μηδὲν ἥδιστος βίος.[2]

The philosophers of the *Old Testament* find themselves in a like contradiction.

The life of a fool is worse than death[3]

and—

In much wisdom is much grief;
And he that increaseth knowledge increaseth sorrow.[4]

I may remark, however, that a man who has no mental needs, because his intellect is of the narrow and normal amount, is, in the strict
sense of the word, what is called a *philistine*—an expression at first peculiar to the German language, a kind of slang term at the Universities,
afterwards used, by analogy, in a higher sense, though still in its original meaning, as denoting one who is not *a Son of the Muses*. A philistine is and remains ἄμουσος ἀνήρ. I should prefer to take a higher
point of view, and apply the term *philistine* to people who are always

---

[1]Antigone, 1347–8.
[2]Ajax, 554.
[3]Ecclesiasticus, xxii. 11.
[4]Ecclesiastes, i. 18.

seriously occupied with realities which are no realities; but as such a definition would be a transcendental one, and therefore not generally intelligible, it would hardly be in place in the present treatise, which aims at being popular. The other definition can be more easily elucidated, indicating, as it does, satisfactorily enough, the essential nature of all those qualities which distinguish the philistine. He is defined to be *a man without mental needs.* From this it follows, firstly, *in relation to himself,* that he has *no intellectual pleasures;* for, as was remarked before, there are no real pleasures without real needs. The philistine's life is animated by no desire to gain knowledge and insight for their own sake, or to experience that true æsthetic pleasure which is so nearly akin to them. If pleasures of this kind are fashionable, and the philistine finds himself compelled to pay attention to them, he will force himself to do so, but he will take as little interest in them as possible. His only real pleasures are of a sensual kind, and he thinks that these indemnify him for the loss of the others. To him oysters and champagne are the height of existence; the aim of his life is to procure what will contribute to his bodily welfare, and he is indeed in a happy way if this causes him some trouble. If the luxuries of life are heaped upon him, he will inevitably be bored, and against boredom he has a great many fancied remedies, balls, theatres, parties, cards, gambling, horses, women, drinking travelling and so on; all of which can not protect a man from being bored, for where there are no intellectual needs, no intellectual pleasures are possible. The peculiar characteristic of the philistine is a dull, dry kind of gravity, akin to that of animals. Nothing really pleases, or excites, or interests him, for sensual pleasure is quickly exhausted, and the society of Philistines soon becomes burdensome, and one may even get tired of playing cards. True, the pleasures of vanity are left, pleasures which he enjoys in his own way, either by feeling himself superior in point of wealth, or rank, or influence and power to other people, who thereupon pay him honour; or, at any rate, by going about with those who have a superfluity of these blessings, sunning himself in the reflection of their splendour—what the English call *a snob.*

From the essential nature of the philistine it follows, secondly, *in regard to others,* that, as he possesses no intellectual, but only physical needs, he will seek the society of those who can satisfy the latter, but not the former. The last thing he will expect from his friends is the possession of any sort of intellectual capacity; nay, if he chances to meet with it, it will rouse his antipathy and even hatred; simply because in addition to an unpleasant sense of inferiority, he experiences, in his heart, a dull kind of envy, which has to be carefully concealed even from himself. Nevertheless, it sometimes grows into a secret feeling of rancour. But for all that, it will never occur to him to make his own ideas of worth or value conform to the standard of such qualities; he will continue to give the preference to rank and riches, power and influence, which in his eyes seem to be the only genuine advantages in the world; and his wish will be to excel in them himself. All this is the consequence of his being a man *without intellectual needs*. The great affliction of all Philistines is that they have no interest in *ideas*, and that, to escape being bored, they are in constant need of *realities*. Now realities are either unsatisfactory or dangerous; when they lose their interest, they become fatiguing. But the ideal world is illimitable and calm,

> something afar
> From the sphere of our sorrow.

Note. — In these remarks on the personal qualities which go to make happiness, I have been mainly concerned with the physical and intellectual nature of man. For an account of the direct and immediate influence of *morality* upon happiness, let me refer to my prize essay on *The Foundation of Morals* (Sec. 22.)

III. PROPERTY, OR WHAT A MAN HAS.

EPICURUS divides the needs of mankind into three classes, and the division made by this great professor of happiness is a true and a fine one. First come natural and necessary needs, such as, when not satisfied, produce pain, — food and clothing, *victus et amictus*, needs which can easily be satisfied. Secondly, there are those needs which, though natural, are not necessary, such as the gratification of certain of the senses. I may add, however, that in the report given by Diogenes Laertius, Epicurus does not mention which of the senses he means; so that on this point my account of his doctrine is somewhat more definite and exact than the original. These are needs rather more difficult to satisfy. The third class consists of needs which are neither natural nor necessary, the need of luxury and prodigality, show and splendour, which never come to an end, and are very hard to satisfy.[1]

It is difficult, if not impossible, to define the limits which reason should impose on the desire for wealth; for there is no absolute or definite amount of wealth which will satisfy a man. The amount is always relative, that is to say, just so much as will maintain the proportion between what he wants and what he gets; for to measure a man's happi-

---

[1] Cf. Diogenes Laertius, Bk. x., ch. xxvii., pp. 127 and 149, also Cicero *de finibus*, i., 13.

ness only by what he gets, and not also by what he expects to get, is as
futile as to try to express a fraction which shall have a numerator but no
denominator. A man never feels the loss of things which it never occurs
to him to ask for; he is just as happy without them; whilst another, who
may have a hundred times as much, feels miserable because he has not
got the one thing which he wants. In fact, here too, every man has an
horizon of his own, and he will expect just as much as he thinks it possible for him to get. If an object within his horizon looks as though he
could confidently reckon on getting it, he is happy; but if difficulties
come in the way, he is miserable. What lies beyond his horizon has no
effect at all upon him. So it is that the vast possessions of the rich do
not agitate the poor, and conversely, that a wealthy man is not consoled
by all his wealth for the failure of his hopes. Riches, one may say, are
like sea-water: the more you drink, the thirstier you become; and the
same is true of fame. The loss of wealth and prosperity leaves a man, as
soon as the first pangs of grief are over, in very much the same habitual
temper as before; and the reason of this is, that as soon as fate dimin-
ishes the amount of his possessions, he himself immediately reduces
the amount of his claims. But when misfortune comes upon us, to re-
duce the amount of our claims is just what is most painful; when once
we have done so, the pain becomes less and less, and is felt no more;
like an old wound which has healed. Conversely, when a piece of good
fortune befalls us, our claims mount higher and higher, as there is
nothing to regulate them. It is in this feeling of expansion that the delight of it lies. But it lasts no longer than the process itself, and when
the expansion is complete, the delight ceases: we have become accustomed to the increase in our claims, and consequently indifferent to
the amount of wealth which satisfies them. There is a passage in the
Odyssey[1] illustrating this truth, of which I may quote the last two lines:

Τοῖος γὰρ νόος ἐστὶν ἐπιχθονίων ἀνθρώπων
Οἶον ἐφ᾽ ἦμαρ ἄγει πατὴρ ἀνδρῶν τε θεῶν τε.

—the thoughts of man that dwells on the earth are as the day granted
him by the father of gods and men. Discontent springs from a constant
endeavour to increase the amount of our claims, when we are power-
less to increase the amount which will satisfy them.

When we consider how full of needs the human race is, how its
whole existence is based upon them, it is not a matter for surprise that
wealth is held in more sincere esteem, nay, in greater honour, than
anything else in the world; nor ought we to wonder that gain is made
the only goal of life, and everything that does not lead to it pushed aside

---

[1] xviii., 130–7.

or thrown overboard—philosophy, for instance, by those who profess it.
People are often reproached for wishing for money above all things,
and for loving it more than anything else; but it is natural and even inevitable for people to love that which, like an unwearied Proteus, is always ready to turn itself into whatever object their wandering wishes or
manifold desires may for the moment fix upon. Everything else can satisfy only *one* wish, *one* need: food is good only if you are hungry; wine,
if you are able to enjoy it; drugs, if you are sick; fur for the winter; love
for youth, and so on. These are all only relatively good, ἀγαθὰ πρός
τι. Money alone is absolutely good, because it is not only a concrete
satisfaction of one need in particular; it is an abstract satisfaction of all.

If a man has an independent fortune, he should regard it as a bulwark against the many evils and misfortunes which he may encounter;
he should not look upon it as giving him leave to get what pleasure he
can out of the world, or as rendering it incumbent upon him to spend
it in this way. People who are not born with a fortune, but end by making a large one through the exercise of whatever talents they possess, almost always come to think that their talents are their capital, and that
the money they have gained is merely the interest upon it; they do not
lay by a part of their earnings to form permanent capital, but spend
their money much as they have earned it. Accordingly, they often fall
into poverty: their earnings decrease, or come to an end altogether, either because their talent is exhausted by becoming antiquated,—as, for
instance, very often happens in the case of fine art—or else it was valid
only under a special conjunction of circumstances which has now
passed away. There is nothing to prevent those who live on the common labour of their hands from treating their earnings in that way if
they like; because their kind of skill is not likely to disappear, or, if it
does, it can be replaced by that of their fellow-workmen; moreover, the
kind of work they do is always in demand; so that what the proverb says
is quite true, *a useful trade is a mine of gold.* But with artists and pro-
fessionals of every kind the case is quite different, and that is the reason
why they are well paid. They ought to build up a capital out of their
earnings; but they recklessly look upon them as merely interest, and
end in ruin. On the other hand, people who inherit money know, at
least, how to distinguish between capital and interest, and most of them
try to make their capital secure and not encroach upon it; nay, if they
can, they put by at least an eighth of their interest in order to meet future contingencies. So most of them maintain their position. These few
remarks about capital and interest are not applicable to commercial
life, for merchants look upon money only as a means of further gain,
just as a workman regards his tools; so even if their capital has been entirely the result of their own efforts, they try to preserve and increase it

by using it. Accordingly, wealth is nowhere so much at home as in the merchant class.

It will generally be found that those who know what it is to have been in need and destitution are very much less afraid of it, and consequently more inclined to extravagance, than those who know poverty only by hearsay. People who have been born and bred in good circumstances are as a rule much more careful about the future, more economical, in fact, than those who by a piece of good luck, have suddenly passed from poverty to wealth. This looks as if poverty were not really such a very wretched thing as it appears from a distance. The true reason, however, is rather the fact that the man who has been born into a position of wealth comes to look upon it as something without which he could no more live than he could live without air; he guards it as he does his very life; and so he is generally a lover of order, prudent and economical. But the man who has been born into a poor position looks upon it as the natural one, and if by any chance he comes in for a fortune, he regards it as a superfluity, something to be enjoyed or wasted, because, if it comes to an end, he can get on just as well as before, with one anxiety the less; or, as Shakespeare says in Henry VI.,[1]

> . . . the adage must be verified
> That beggars mounted run their horse to death.

But it should be said that people of this kind have a firm and excessive trust, partly in fate, partly in the peculiar means which have already raised them out of need and poverty,—a trust not only of the head, but of the heart also; and so they do not, like the man born rich, look upon the shallows of poverty as bottomless, but console themselves with the thought that when they have touched ground again, they can take another upward flight. It is this trait in human character which explains the fact that women who were poor before their marriage often make greater claims, and are more extravagant, than those who have brought their husbands a rich dowry; because as a rule, rich girls bring with them, not only a fortune, but also more eagerness, nay, more of the inherited instinct, to preserve it, than poor girls do. If anyone doubts the truth of this, and thinks that it is just the opposite, he will find authority for his view in Ariosto's first Satire; but, on the other hand, Dr. Johnson agrees with my opinion. *A woman of fortune*, he says, *being used to the handling of money, spends it judiciously; but a woman who gets the command of money for the first time upon her marriage, has such a gusto in spending it, that she throws it away with great profusion.*[2]

---

[1]Part III., Act 1, Sc. 4.
[2]Boswell's Life of Johnson: ann; 1776, ætat: 67.

And in any case let me advise anyone who marries a poor girl not to leave her the capital but only the interest, and to take especial care that she has not the management of the children's fortune.

I do not by any means think that I am touching upon a subject which is not worth my while to mention when I recommend people to be careful to preserve what they have earned or inherited. For to start life with just as much as will make one independent, that is, allow one to live comfortably without having to work—even if one has only just enough for oneself, not to speak of a family—is an advantage which cannot be over-estimated; for it means exemption and immunity from that chronic disease of penury, which fastens on the life of man like a plague; it is emancipation from that forced labour which is the natural lot of every mortal. Only under a favourable fate like this can a man be said to be born free, to be, in the proper sense of the word, *sui juris*, master of his own time and powers, and able to say every morning, *This day is my own.* And just for the same reason the difference between the man who has a hundred a year and the man who has a thousand, is infinitely smaller than the difference between the former and a man who has nothing at all. But inherited wealth reaches its utmost value when it falls to the individual endowed with mental powers of a high order, who is resolved to pursue a line of life not compatible with the making of money; for he is then doubly endowed by fate and can live for his genius; and he will pay his debt to mankind a hundred times, by achieving what no other could achieve, by producing some work which contributes to the general good, and redounds to the honour of humanity at large. Another, again, may use his wealth to further philanthropic schemes, and make himself well-deserving of his fellow-men. But a man who does none of these things, who does not even try to do them, who never attempts to study thoroughly some one branch of knowledge so that he may at least do what he can towards promoting it—such a one, born as he is into riches, is a mere idler and thief of time, a contemptible fellow. He will not even be happy, because, in his ease, exemption from need delivers him up to the other extreme of human suffering, boredom, which is such martyrdom to him, that he would have been better off if poverty had given him something to do. And as he is bored he is apt to be extravagant, and so lose the advantage of which he showed himself unworthy. Countless numbers of people find themselves in want, simply because, when they had money, they spent it only to get momentary relief from the feeling of boredom which oppressed them.

It is quite another matter if one's object is success in political life, where favour, friends and connections are all-important, in order to mount by their aid step by step on the ladder of promotion, and per-

haps gain the topmost rung. In this kind of life, it is much better to be
cast on the world without a penny; and if the aspirant is not of noble
family, but is a man of some talent, it will redound to his advantage to
be an absolute pauper. For what every one most aims at in ordinary
contact with his fellows is to prove them inferior to himself; and how
much more is this the case in politics. Now, it is only an absolute pauper who has such a thorough conviction of his own complete, profound
and positive inferiority from every point of view, of his own utter in-
significance and worthlessness, that he can take his place quietly in the
political machine.[1] He is the only one who can keep on bowing low
enough, and even go right down upon his face if necessary; he alone
can submit to everything and laugh at it; he alone knows the entire
worthlessness of merit; he alone uses his loudest voice and his boldest
type whenever he has to speak or write of those who are placed over his
head, or occupy any position of influence; and if they do a little scrib-
bling, he is ready to applaud it as a masterwork. He alone understands
how to beg, and so betimes, when he is hardly out of his boyhood, he
becomes a high priest of that hidden mystery which Goethe brings to
light;—

> Ueber's Niederträchtige
> Niemand sich beklage:
> Denn es ist das Mächtige
> Was man dir auch sage:

—it is no use to complain of low aims; for, whatever people may say,
they rule the world.

On the other hand, the man who is born with enough to live upon
is generally of a somewhat independent turn of mind; he is accustomed
to keep his head up; he has not learned all the arts of the beggar; perhaps he even presumes a little upon the possession of talents which, as
he ought to know, can never compete with cringing mediocrity; in the
long run he comes to recognise the inferiority of those who are placed
over his head, and when they try to put insults upon him, he becomes
refractory and shy. This is not the way to get on in the world. Nay, such
a man may at last incline to the opinion freely expressed by Voltaire:
*We have only two days to live; it is not worth our while to spend them in
cringing to contemptible rascals.* But alas! let me observe by the way,
that *contemptible rascal* is an attribute which may be predicated of an

---

[1]*Translator's Note.*—Schopenhauer is probably here making one of his many virulent
attacks upon Hegel; in this case on account of what he thought to be the philosopher's
abject servility to the government of his day. Though the Hegelian system has been the
fruitful mother of many liberal ideas, there can be no doubt that Hegel's influence, in
his own life-time, was an effective support of Prussian bureaucracy.

abominable number of people. What Juvenal says—it is difficult to rise if your poverty is greater than your talent—

> Haud facile emergunt quorum virtutibus obstat
> Res angusta domi—

is more applicable to a career of art and literature than to political and social ambition.

Wife and children I have not reckoned amongst a man's possessions: he is rather in their possession. It would be easier to include friends under that head; but a man's friends belong to him not a whit more than he belongs to them.

IV. POSITION, OR A MAN'S PLACE IN THE ESTIMATION OF OTHERS.

Section 1.—Reputation.

BY A peculiar weakness of human nature, people generally think too much about the opinion which others form of them; although the slightest reflection will show that this opinion, whatever it may be, is not in itself essential to happiness. Therefore it is hard to understand why everybody feels so very pleased when he sees that other people have a good opinion of him, or say anything flattering to his vanity. If you stroke a cat, it will purr; and, as inevitably, if you praise a man, a sweet expression of delight will appear on his face; and even though the praise is a palpable lie, it will be welcome, if the matter is one on which he prides himself. If only other people will applaud him, a man may console himself for downright misfortune, or for the pittance he gets from the two sources of human happiness already discussed; and conversely, it is astonishing how infallibly a man will be annoyed, and in some cases deeply pained, by any wrong done to his feeling of self-importance, whatever be the nature, degree, or circumstances of the injury, or by any depreciation, slight, or disregard.

If the feeling of honour rests upon this peculiarity of human nature, it may have a very salutary effect upon the welfare of a great many people, as a substitute for morality; but upon their happiness, more especially upon that peace of mind and independence which are so essential to happiness, its effect will be disturbing and prejudicial rather than salutary. Therefore it is advisable, from our point of view, to set limits to this weakness, and duly to consider and rightly to estimate the relative value of advantages, and thus temper, as far as possible, this great susceptibility to other people's opinion, whether the opinion be one flattering to our vanity, or whether it causes us pain; for in either case it is the same feeling which is touched. Otherwise, a man is the slave of what other people are pleased to think,—and how little it requires to disconcert or soothe the mind that is greedy of praise:—

> Sic leve, sic parvum est, animum quod laudis avarum
> Subruit ac reficit.[1]

Therefore it will very much conduce to our happiness if we duly compare the value of what a man is in and for himself with what he is in the eyes of others. Under the former comes everything that fills up the span of our existence and makes it what it is, in short, all the advantages already considered and summed up under the heads of personality and property; and the sphere in which all this takes place is the man's own consciousness. On the other hand, the sphere of what we are for other people is their consciousness, not ours; it is the kind of figure we make in their eyes, together with the thoughts which this arouses.[2] But this is something which has no direct and immediate existence for us, but can affect us only mediately and indirectly, so far, that is, as other people's behaviour towards us is directed by it; and even then it ought to affect us only in so far as it can move us to modify *what we are in and for ourselves.* Apart from this, what goes on in other people's consciousness is, as such, a matter of indifference to us: and in time we get really indifferent to it, when we come to see how superficial and futile are most people's thoughts, how narrow their ideas, how mean their sentiments, how perverse their opinions, and how much of error there is in most of them; when we learn by experience with what depreciation a man will speak of his fellow, when he is not obliged to fear him, or thinks that what he says will not come to his ears. And if ever we have had an opportunity of seeing how the greatest of men will meet with nothing but slight from half-a-dozen blockheads, we shall understand that to lay great value upon what other people say is to pay them too much honour.

At all events, a man is in a very bad way, who finds no source of happiness in the first two classes of blessings already treated of, but has to seek it in the third, in other words, not in what he is in himself, but in what he is in the opinion of others. For, after all, the foundation of our whole nature, and, therefore, of our happiness, is our physique, and the most essential factor in happiness is health, and, next in importance after health, the ability to maintain ourselves in independence and

---

[1]Horace, Epist: II, 1, 180.
[2]Let me remark that people in the highest positions in life, with all their brilliance, pomp, display, magnificence and general show, may well say:—Our happiness lies entirely outside us, for it exists only in the heads of others.

freedom from care. There can be no competition or compensation between these essential factors on the one side, and honour, pomp, rank and reputation on the other, however much value we may set upon the latter. No one would hesitate to sacrifice the latter for the former, if it were necessary. We should add very much to our happiness by a timely recognition of the simple truth that every man's chief and real existence is in his own skin, and not in other people's opinions; and, consequently, that the actual conditions of our personal life,—health, temperament, capacity, income, wife, children, friends, home, are a hundred times more important for our happiness than what other people are pleased to think of us; otherwise we shall be miserable. And if people insist that honour is dearer than life itself, what they really mean is that existence and well-being are as nothing compared with other people's opinions. Of course, this may be only an exaggerated way of stating the prosaic truth that reputation, that is, the opinion others have of us, is indispensable if we are to make any progress in the world; but I shall come back to that presently. When we see that almost everything men devote their lives to attain, sparing no effort and encountering a thousand toils and dangers in the process, has, in the end, no further object than to raise themselves in the estimation of others; when we see that not only offices, titles, decorations, but also wealth, nay, even knowledge[1] and art, are striven for only to obtain, as the ultimate goal of all effort, greater respect from one's fellow-men,—is not this a lamentable proof of the extent to which human folly can go? To set much too high a value on other people's opinion is a common error everywhere; an error, it may be, rooted in human nature itself, or the result of civilisation and social arrangements generally; but, whatever its source, it exercises a very immoderate influence on all we do, and is very prejudicial to our happiness. We can trace it from a timorous and slavish regard for what other people will say, up to the feeling which made Virginius plunge the danger into his daughter's heart, or induces many a man to sacrifice quiet, riches, health and even life itself, for posthumous glory. Undoubtedly this feeling is a very convenient instrument in the hands of those who have the control or direction of their fellow-men; and accordingly we find that in every scheme for training up humanity in the way it should go, the maintenance and strengthening of the feeling of honour occupies an important place. But it is quite a different matter in its effect on human happiness, of which it is here our object to treat; and we should rather be careful to dissuade people from setting too much store by what others think of

---

[1] *Scire tuum nihil est nisi te scire hoc sciat alter*, (Persius i. 27)—knowledge is no use unless others know that you have it.

them. Daily experience shows us, however, that this is just the mistake people persist in making; most men set the utmost value precisely on what other people think, and are more concerned about it than about what goes on in their own consciousness, which is the thing most immediately and directly present to them. They reverse the natural order, — regarding the opinions of others as real existence and their own consciousness as something shadowy; making the derivative and secondary into the principal, and considering the picture they present to the world of more importance than their own selves. By thus trying to get a direct and immediate result out of what has no really direct or immediate existence, they fall into the kind of folly which is called *vanity* — the appropriate term for that which has no solid or intrinsic value. Like a miser, such people forget the end in their eagerness to obtain the means.

The truth is that the value we set upon the opinion of others, and our constant endeavour in respect of it, are each quite out of proportion to any result we may reasonably hope to attain; so that this attention to other people's attitude may be regarded as a kind of universal mania which everyone inherits. In all we do, almost the first thing we think about is: What will people say; and nearly half the troubles and bothers of life may be traced to our anxiety on this score; it is the anxiety which is at the bottom of all that feeling of self-importance, which is so often mortified because it is so very morbidly sensitive. It is solicitude about what others will say that underlies all our vanity and pretension, yes, and all our show and swagger too. Without it, there would not be a tenth part of the luxury which exists. Pride in every form, *point d'honneur* and *punctilio*, however varied their kind or sphere, are at bottom nothing but this — anxiety about what others will say — and what sacrifices it often costs! One can see it even in a child; and though it exists at every period of life, it is strongest in age; because, when the capacity for sensual pleasure fails, vanity and pride have only avarice to share their dominion. Frenchmen, perhaps, afford the best example of this feeling, and amongst them it is a regular epidemic, appearing sometimes in the most absurd ambition, or in a ridiculous kind of national vanity and the most shameless boasting. However, they frustrate their own aims, for other people make fun of them and call them *la grande nation.*

By way of specially illustrating this perverse and exuberant respect for other people's opinion, let me take a passage from the *Times* of March 31st, 1846, giving a detailed account of the execution of one Thomas Wix, an apprentice who, from motives of vengeance, had murdered his master. Here we have very unusual circumstances and an extraordinary character, though one very suitable for our purpose; and these combine to give a striking picture of this folly, which is so deeply rooted in human nature, and allow us to form an accurate notion of the extent to which it will go. On the morning of the execution, says the report, *the rev. ordinary was early in attendance upon him, but Wix, beyond a quiet demeanour, betrayed no interest in his ministrations, appearing to feel anxious only to acquit himself "bravely" before the spectators of his ignominious end. . . . In the procession Wix fell into his proper place with alacrity, and, as he entered the Chapel-yard, remarked, sufficiently loud to be heard by several persons near him, "Now, then, as Dr. Dodd said, I shall soon know the grand secret." On reaching the scaffold, the miserable wretch mounted the drop without the slightest assistance, and when he got to the centre, he bowed to the spectators twice, a proceeding which called forth a tremendous cheer from the degraded crowd beneath.*

This is an admirable example of the way in which a man, with death in the most dreadful form before his very eyes, and eternity beyond it, will care for nothing but the impression he makes upon a crowd of gapers, and the opinion he leaves behind him in their heads. There was much the same kind of thing in the case of Lecomte, who was executed at Frankfurt, also in 1846, for an attempt on the king's life. At the trial he was very much annoyed that he was not allowed to appear, in decent attire, before the Upper House; and on the day of the execution it was a special grief to him that he was not permitted to shave. It is not only in recent times that this kind of thing has been known to happen. Mateo Aleman tells us, in the Introduction to his celebrated romance, *Guzman de Alfarache*, that many infatuated criminals, instead of devoting their last hours to the welfare of their souls, as they ought to have done, neglect this duty for the purpose of preparing and committing to memory a speech to be made from the scaffold.

I take these extreme cases as being the best illustrations of what I mean; for they give us a magnified reflection of our own nature. The anxieties of all of us, our worries, vexations, bothers, troubles, uneasy apprehensions and strenuous efforts are due, in perhaps the large majority of instances, to what other people will say; and we are just as foolish in this respect as those miserable criminals. Envy and hatred are very often traceable to a similar source.

Now, it is obvious that happiness, which consists for the most part in peace of mind and contentment, would be served by nothing so much as by reducing this impulse of human nature within reasonable limits,—which would perhaps make it one fiftieth part of what it is now. By doing so, we should get rid of a thorn in the flesh which is always causing us pain. But it is a very difficult task, because the impulse in question is a natural and innate perversity of human nature. Tacitus says, *The lust of fame is the last that a wise man shakes off.*[1] The only way of putting an end to this universal folly is to see clearly that it is a folly; and this may be done by recognising the fact that most of the opinions in men's heads are apt to be false, perverse, erroneous and absurd, and so in themselves unworthy of any attention; further, that other people's opinions can have very little real and positive influence upon us in most of the circumstances and affairs of life. Again, this opinion is generally of such an unfavourable character that it would worry a man to death to hear everything that was said of him, or the tone in which he was spoken of. And finally, among other things, we should be clear about the fact that honour itself has no really direct, but only an indirect, value. If people were generally converted from this universal folly, the result would be such an addition to our peace of mind and cheerfulness as at present seems inconceivable; people would present a firmer and more confident front to the world, and generally behave with less embarrassment and restraint. It is observable that a retired mode of life has an exceedingly beneficial influence on our peace of mind, and this is mainly because we thus escape having to live constantly in the sight of others, and pay everlasting regard to their casual opinions; in a word, we are able to return upon ourselves. At the same time a good deal of positive misfortune might be avoided, which we are now drawn into by striving after shadows, or, to speak more correctly, by indulging a mischievous piece of folly; and we should consequently have more attention to give to solid realities and enjoy them with less interruption than at present. But χαλεπὰ τὰ καλὰ—what is worth doing is hard to do.

Section 2.—Pride.

The folly of our nature which we are discussing puts forth three shoots, ambition, vanity and pride. The difference between the last two is this: *pride* is an established conviction of one's own paramount worth in some particular respect; while *vanity* is the desire of rousing such a conviction in others, and it is generally accompanied by the secret hope of ultimately coming to the same conviction oneself. Pride works *from within;* it is the direct appreciation of oneself. Vanity is the desire to arrive at this appreciation indirectly, *from without.* So we find that vain people are talkative, and proud, taciturn. But the vain person ought to be aware that the good opinion of others, which he strives for, may be obtained much more easily and certainly by persistent silence than by speech, even though he has very good things to say. Anyone

---

[1]Hist., iv., 6.

who wishes to affect pride is not therefore a proud man; but he will soon have to drop this, as every other, assumed character.

It is only a firm, unshakeable conviction of preeminent worth and special value which makes a man proud in the true sense of the word,—a conviction which may, no doubt, be a mistaken one or rest on advantages which are of an adventitious and conventional character: still pride is not the less pride for all that, so long as it be present in real earnest. And since pride is thus rooted in conviction, it resembles every other form of knowledge in not being within our own arbitrament. Pride's worst foe,—I mean its greatest obstacle,—is vanity, which courts the applause of the world in order to gain the necessary foundation for a high opinion of one's own worth, whilst pride is based upon a pre-existing conviction of it.

It is quite true that pride is something which is generally found fault with, and cried down; but usually, I imagine, by those who have nothing upon which they can pride themselves. In view of the impudence and foolhardiness of most people, anyone who possesses any kind of superiority or merit will do well to keep his eyes fixed on it, if he does not want it to be entirely forgotten; for if a man is good-natured enough to ignore his own privileges, and hob-nob with the generality of other people, as if he were quite on their level, they will be sure to treat him, frankly and candidly, as one of themselves. This is a piece of advice I would specially offer to those who superiority is of the highest kind— eal superiority, I mean, of a purely personal nature—which cannot, like orders and titles, appeal to the eye or ear at every moment; as, otherwise, they will find that familiarity breeds contempt, or, as the Romans used to say, *sus Minervam. Joke with a slave, and he'll soon show his heels*, is an excellent Arabian proverb; nor ought we to despise what Horase says,

> Sume superbiam
> Quœsitam meritis.

—usurp the fame you have deserved. No doubt, when modesty was made a virtue, it was a very advantageous thing for the fools; for everybody is expected to speak of himself as if he were one. This is levelling down indeed! for it comes to look as if there were nothing but fools in the world.

The cheapest sort of pride is national pride; for if a man is proud of his own nation, it argues that he has no qualities of his own of which he can be proud; otherwise, he would not have recourse to those which he shares with so many millions of his fellow-men. The man who is endowed with important personal qualities will be only too ready to see clearly in what respects his own nation falls short, since their failings will be constantly before his eyes. But every miserable fool who has nothing at all of which he can be proud adopts, as a last resource, pride in the nation to which he belongs; he is ready and glad to defend all its faults and follies tooth and nail, thus re-imbursing himself for his own inferiority. For example, if you speak of the stupid and degrading bigotry of the English nation with the contempt it deserves, you will hardly find one Englishman in fifty to agree with you; but if there should be one, he will generally happen to be an intelligent man.

The Germans have no national pride, which shows how honest they are, as everybody knows! and how dishonest are those who, by a piece of ridiculous affectation, pretend that they are proud of their country—the *Deutsche Brüder* and the demagogues who flatter the mob in order to mislead it. I have heard it said that gunpowder was invented by a German. I doubt it. Lichtenberg asks, *Why is it that a man who is not a German does not care about pretending that he is one; and that if he makes any pretence at all, it is to be a Frenchman or an Englishman?*[1]

However that may be, individuality is a far more important thing than nationality, and in any given man deserves a thousand-fold more consideration. And since you cannot speak of national character without referring to large masses of people, it is impossible to be loud in your praises and at the same time honest. National character is only another name for the particular form which the littleness, perversity and baseness of mankind take in every country. If we become disgusted with one, we praise another, until we get disgusted with this too. Every nation mocks at other nations, and all are right.

The contents of this chapter, which treats, as I have said, of what we represent in the world, or what we are in the eyes of others, may be further distributed under three heads: honour, rank and fame.

Section 3.—Rank.

Let us take rank first, as it may be dismissed in a few words, although it plays an important part in the eyes of the masses and of the Philistines, and is a most useful wheel in the machinery of the State.

It has a purely conventional value. Strictly speaking, it is a sham; its method is to exact an artificial respect, and, as a matter of fact, the whole thing is a mere farce.

Orders, it may be said, are bills of exchange drawn on public opinion, and the measure of their value is the credit of the drawer. Of

---

[1] *Translator's Note.* It should be remembered that these remarks were written in the earlier part of the present century, and that a German philosopher now-a-days, even though he were as apt to say bitter things as Schopenhauer, could hardly write in a similar strain.

course, as a substitute for pensions, they save the State a good deal of money; and, besides, they serve a very useful purpose, if they are distributed with discrimination and judgment. For people in general have eyes and ears, it is true; but not much else, very little judgment indeed, or even memory. There are many services to the State quite beyond the range of their understanding; others, again, are appreciated and made much of for a time, and then soon forgotten. It seems to me, therefore, very proper, that a cross or a star should proclaim to the mass of people always and everywhere, *This man is not like you; he has done something.* But orders lose their value when they are distributed unjustly, or without due selection, or in too great numbers: a prince should be as careful in conferring them as a man of business is in signing a bill. It is a pleonasm to inscribe on any order *for distinguished service;* for every order ought to be for distinguished service. That stands to reason.

Section 4.—Honour.

Honour is a much larger question than rank, and more difficult to discuss. Let us begin by trying to define it.

If I were to say *Honour is external conscience, and conscience is inward honour,* no doubt a good many people would assent; but there would be more show than reality about such a definition, and it would hardly go to the root of the matter. I prefer to say, *Honour is, on its objective side, other people's opinion of what we are worth; on its subjective side, it is the respect we pay to this opinion.* From the latter point of view, to be *a man of honour* is to exercise what is often a very wholesome, but by no means a purely moral, influence.

The feelings of honour and shame exist in every man who is not utterly depraved, and honour is everywhere recognised as something particularly valuable. The reason of this is as follows. By and in himself a man can accomplish very little; he is like Robinson Crusoe on a desert island. It is only in society that a man's powers can be called into full activity. He very soon finds this out when his consciousness begins to develop, and there arises in him the desire to be looked upon as a useful member of society, as one, that is, who is capable of playing his part as a man—*pro parte virili*—thereby acquiring a right to the benefits of social life. Now, to be a useful member of society, one must do two things: firstly, what everyone is expected to do everywhere; and, secondly, what one's own particular position in the world demands and requires.

But a man soon discovers that everything depends upon his being useful, not in his own opinion, but in the opinion of others; and so he tries his best to make that favourable impression upon the world, to which he attaches such a high value. Hence, this primitive and innate characteristic of human nature, which is called the feeling of honour, or, under another aspect, the feeling of shame—*verecundia*. It is this which brings a blush to his cheek at the thought of having suddenly to fall in the estimation of others, even when he knows that he is innocent, nay, even if his remissness extends to no absolute obligation, but only to one which he has taken upon himself of his own free will. Conversely, nothing in life gives a man so much courage as the attainment or renewal of the conviction that other people regard him with favour; because it means that everyone joins to give him help and protection, which is an infinitely stronger bulwark against the ills of life than anything he can do himself.

The variety of relations in which a man can stand to other people so as to obtain their confidence, that is, their good opinion, gives rise to a distinction between several kinds of honour, resting chiefly on the different bearings that *meum* may take to *tuum*; or, again, on the performance of various pledges; or finally, on the relation of the sexes. Hence, there are three main kinds of honour, each of which takes various forms—civic honour, official honour, and sexual honour.

Civic honour has the widest sphere of all. It consists in the assumption that we shall pay unconditional respect to the rights of others, and, therefore, never use any unjust or unlawful means of getting what we want. It is the condition of all peaceable intercourse between man and man; and it is destroyed by anything that openly and manifestly militates against this peaceable intercourse, anything, accordingly, which entails punishment at the hands of the law, always supposing that the punishment is a just one.

The ultimate foundation of honour is the conviction that moral character is unalterable: a single bad action implies that future actions of the same kind will, under similar circumstances, also be bad. This is well expressed by the English use of the word *character* as meaning credit, reputation, honour. Hence honour, once lost, can never be recovered; unless the loss rested on some mistake, such as may occur if a man is slandered or his actions viewed in a false light. So the law provides remedies against slander, libel, and even insult; for insult, though it amount to no more than mere abuse, is a kind of summary slander with a suppression of the reasons. What I mean may be well put in the Greek phrase—not quoted from any author—ἔστιν ἡ λοιδορία διαβολὴ σύντομος. It is true that if a man abuses another, he is simply showing that he has no real or true causes of complaint against him; as, otherwise, he would bring these forward as the premises, and rely upon his hearers to draw the conclusion themselves; instead of which, he gives the conclusion and leaves out the premises, trusting that people will suppose that he has done so only for the sake of being brief.

Civic honour draws its existence and name from the middle classes; but it applies equally to all, not excepting the highest. No man can disregard it, and it is a very serious thing, of which every one should be careful not to make light. The man who breaks confidence has for ever forfeited confidence, whatever he may do, and whoever he may be; and the bitter consequences of the loss of confidence can never be averted.

There is a sense in which honour may be said to have a *negative* character in opposition to the *positive* character of fame. For honour is not the opinion people have of particular qualities which a man may happen to possess exclusively; it is rather the opinion they have of the qualities which a man may be expected to exhibit, and to which he should not prove false. Honour, therefore, means that a man is not exceptional; fame, that he is. Fame is something which must be won; honour, only something which must not be lost. The absence of fame is obscurity, which is only a negative; but loss of honour is shame, which is a positive quality. This negative character of honour must not be confused with anything *passive* for honour is above all things active in its working. It is the only quality which proceeds *directly* from the man who exhibits it: it is concerned entirely with what he does and leaves undone, and has nothing to do with the actions of others or the obstacles they place in his way. It is something entirely in our own power—τῶν ἐφ'ἡμῶν. This distinction, as we shall see presently, marks off true honour from the sham honour of chivalry.

Slander is the only weapon by which honour can be attacked from without; and the only way to repel the attack is to confute the slander with the proper amount of publicity, and a due unmasking of him who utters it.

The reason why respect is paid to age is that old people have necessarily shown in the course of their lives whether or not they have been able to maintain their honour unblemished; while that of young people has not yet been put to the proof, though they are credited with the possession of it. For neither length of years,—equalled, as it is, and even excelled, in the case of some of the lower animals,—nor, again, experience, which is only a closer knowledge of the world's ways, can be any sufficient reason for the respect which the young are everywhere required to show towards the old: for if it were merely a matter of years, the weakness which attends on age would call rather for consideration than for respect. It is, however, a remarkable fact that white hair always commands reverence—a reverence really innate and instinctive. Wrinkles—a much surer sign of old age—command no reverence at all: you never hear any one speak of *venerable wrinkles*; but *venerable white hair* is a common expression.

Honour has only an indirect value. For, as I explained at the beginning of this chapter, what other people think of us, if it affects us at all, can affect us only in so far as it governs their behaviour towards us, and only just so long as we live with, or have to do with, them. But it is to society alone that we owe that safety which we and our possessions enjoy in a state of civilisation; in all we do we need the help of others, and they, in their turn, must have confidence in us before they can have anything to do with us. Accordingly, their opinion of us is, indirectly, a matter of great importance; though I cannot see how it can have a direct or immediate value. This is an opinion also held by Cicero. *I quite agree,* he writes, *with what Chrysippus and Diogenes used to say, that a good reputation is not worth raising a finger to obtain, if it were not that it is so useful.*[1] This truth has been insisted upon at great length by Helvetius in his chief work *De l'Esprit,*[2] the conclusion of which is that *we love esteem not for its own sake, but solely for the advantages which it brings.* And as the means can never be more than the end, that saying, of which so much is made, *Honour is dearer than life itself,* is, as I have remarked, a very exaggerated statement. So much, then, for civic honour.

Official honour is the general opinion of other people that a man who fills any office really has the necessary qualities for the proper discharge of all the duties which appertain to it. The greater and more important the duties a man has to discharge in the State, and the higher and more influential the office which he fills, the stronger must be the opinion which people have of the moral and intellectual qualities which render him fit for his post. Therefore, the higher his position, the greater must be the degree of honour paid to him, expressed, as it is, in titles, orders and the generally subservient behaviour of others towards him. As a rule, a man's official rank implies the particular degree of honour which ought to be paid to him, however much this degree may be modified by the capacity of the masses to form any notion of its importance. Still, as a matter of fact, greater honour is paid to a man who fulfils special duties than to the common citizen, whose honour mainly consists in keeping clear of dishonour.

Official honour demands, further, that the man who occupies an office must maintain respect for it, for the sake both of his colleagues and of those who will come after him. This respect an official can maintain by a proper observance of his duties, and by repelling any attack that

[1]*De finibus* iii., 17.
[2]*Disc:* iii., 13.

may be made upon the office itself or upon its occupant: he must not, for instance, pass over unheeded any statement to the effect that the duties of the office are not properly discharged, or that the office itself does not conduce to the public welfare. He must prove the unwarrantable nature of such attacks by enforcing the legal penalty for them.

Subordinate to the honour of official personages comes that of those who serve the State in any other capacity, as doctors, lawyers, teachers, anyone, in short, who by graduating in any subject, or by any other public declaration that he is qualified to exercise some special skill, claims to practise it; in a word, the honour of all those who take any public pledges whatever. Under this head comes military honour, in the true sense of the word, the opinion that people who have bound themselves to defend their country really possess the requisite qualities which will enable them to do so, especially courage, personal bravery and strength, and that they are perfectly ready to defend their country to the death, and never and under no circumstances desert the flag to which they have once sworn allegiance. I have here taken official honour in a wider sense than that in which it is generally used, namely, the respect due by citizens to an office itself.

In treating of *sexual honour* and the principles on which it rests, a little more attention and analysis are necessary; and what I shall say will support my contention that all honour really rests upon a utilitarian basis. There are two natural divisions of the subject—the honour of women and the honour of men, in either side issuing in a well-understood *esprit de corps*. The former is by far the more important of the two, because the most essential feature in woman's life is her relation to man.

Female honour is the general opinion in regard to a girl that she is pure, and in regard to a wife that she is faithful. The importance of this opinion rests upon the following considerations. Women depend upon men in all the relations of life; men upon women, it might be said, in one only. So an arrangement is made for mutual interdependence— man undertaking responsibility for all woman's needs and also for the children that spring from their union—an arrangement on which is based the welfare of the whole female race. To carry out this plan, women have to band together with a show of *esprit de corps*, and present one undivided front to their common enemy, man,—who possesses all the good things of the earth, in virtue of his superior physical and intellectual power,—in order to lay siege to and conquer him, and so get possession of him and a share of those good things. To this end the honour of all women depends upon the enforcement of the rule that no woman should give herself to a man except in marriage, in order that every man may be forced, as it were, to surrender and ally himself with a woman; by this arrangement provision is made for the whole of the female race. This is a result, however, which can be obtained only by a strict observance of the rule; and, accordingly, women everywhere show true *esprit de corps* in carefully insisting upon its maintenance. Any girl who commits a breach of the rule betrays the whole female race, because its welfare would be destroyed if every woman were to do likewise; so she is cast out with shame as one who has lost her honour. No woman will have anything more to do with her; she is avoided like the plague. The same doom is awarded to a woman who breaks the marriage tie; for in so doing she is false to the terms upon which the man capitulated; and as her conduct is such as to frighten other men from making a similar surrender, it imperils the welfare of all her sisters. Nay more; this deception and coarse breach of troth is a crime punishable by the loss, not only of personal, but also of civic honour. This is why we minimise the shame of a girl, but not of a wife; because, in the former case, marriage can restore honour, while in the latter, no atonement can be made for the breach of contract.

Once this *esprit de corps* is acknowledged to be the foundation of female honour, and is seen to be a wholesome, nay, a necessary arrangement, as at bottom a matter of prudence and interest, its extreme importance for the welfare of women will be recognised. But it does not possess anything more than a relative value. It is no absolute end, lying beyond all other aims of existence and valued above life itself. In this view, there will be nothing to applaud in the forced and extravagant conduct of a Lucretia or a Virginius—conduct which can easily degenerate into tragic farce, and produce a terrible feeling of revulsion. The conclusion of *Emilia Galotti*, for instance, makes one leave the theatre completely ill at ease; and, on the other hand, all the rules of female honour cannot prevent a certain sympathy with Clara in *Egmont*. To carry this principle of female honour too far is to forget the end in thinking of the means—and this is just what people often do; for such exaggeration suggests that the value of sexual honour is absolute; while the truth is that it is more relative than any other kind. One might go so far as to say that its value is purely conventional, when one sees from Thomasius how in all ages and countries, up to the time of the Reformation, irregularities were permitted and recognised by law, with no derogation to female honour,—not to speak of the temple of Mylitta at Babylon.[1]

There are also, of course, certain circumstances in civil life which make external forms of marriage impossible, especially in Catholic countries, where there is no such thing as divorce. Ruling princes

---

[1] Herodotus, i., 199.

everywhere, would, in my opinion, do much better, from a moral point of view, to dispense with forms altogether rather than contract a morganatic marriage, the descendants of which might raise claims to the throne if the legitimate stock happened to die out; so that there is a possibility, though, perhaps, a remote one, that a morganatic marriage might produce a civil war. And, besides, such a marriage, concluded in defiance of all outward ceremony, is a concession made to women and priests—two classes of persons to whom one should be most careful to give as little tether as possible. It is further to be remarked that every man in a country can marry the woman of his choice, except one poor individual, namely, the prince. His hand belongs to his country, and can be given in marriage only for reasons of State, that is, for the good of the country. Still, for all that, he is a man; and, as a man, he likes to follow whither his heart leads. It is an unjust, ungrateful and priggish thing to forbid, or to desire to forbid, a prince from following his inclinations in this matter; of course, as long as the lady has no influence upon the Government of the country. From her point of view she occupies an exceptional position, and does not come under the ordinary rules of sexual honour; for she has merely given herself to a man who loves her, and whom she loves but cannot marry. And in general, the fact that the principle of female honour has no origin in nature, is shown by the many bloody sacrifices which have been offered to it,—the murder of children and the mother's suicide. No doubt a girl who contravenes the code commits a breach of faith against her whole sex; but this faith is one which is only secretly taken for granted, and not sworn to. And since, in most cases, her own prospects suffer most immediately, her folly is infinitely greater than her crime.

The corresponding virtue in men is a product of the one I have been discussing. It is their *esprit de corps*, which demands that, when a man has made that surrender of himself in marriage which is so advantageous to his conqueror, he shall take care that the terms of the treaty are maintained; both in order that the agreement itself may lose none of its force by the permission of any laxity in its observance, and that men, having given up everything, may, at least, be assured of their bargain, namely, exclusive possession. Accordingly, it is part of a man's honour to resent a breach of the marriage tie on the part of his wife, and to punish it, at the very least by separating from her. If he condones the offence, his fellow-men cry shame upon him; but the shame in this case is not nearly so foul as that of the woman who has lost her honour; the stain is by no means of so deep a dye—*levioris notae macula;*—because a man's relation to woman is subordinate to many other and more important affairs in his life. The two great dramatic poets of modern times have each taken man's honour as the theme of two plays;

Shakespeare in *Othello* and *The Winter's Tale*, and Calderon in *El medico de su honra*, (the Physician of his Honour), and *A secreto agravio secreta venganza*, (for Secret Insult Secret Vengeance). It should be said, however, that honour demands the punishment of the wife only; to punish her paramour too, is a work of supererogation. This confirms the view I have taken, that a man's honour originates in *esprit de corps*.

The kind of honour which I have been discussing hitherto has always existed in its various forms and principles amongst all nations and at all times; although the history of female honour shows that its principles have undergone certain local modifications at different periods. But there is another species of honour which differs from this entirely, a species of honour of which the Greeks and Romans had no conception, and up to this day it is perfectly unknown amongst Chinese, Hindoos or Mohammedans. It is a kind of honour which arose only in the Middle Age, and is indigenous only to Christian Europe, nay, only to an extremely small portion of the population, that is to say, the higher classes of society and those who ape them. It is *knightly honour*, or *point d'honneur*. Its principles are quite different from those which underlie the kind of honour I have been treating until now, and in some respects are even opposed to them. The sort I am referring to produces the *cavalier*; while the other kind creates the *man of honour*. As this is so, I shall proceed to give an explanation of its principles, as a kind of code or mirror of knightly courtesy.

(1.) To begin with, honour of this sort consists, not in other people's opinion of what we are worth, but wholly and entirely in whether they express it or not, no matter whether they really have any opinion at all, let alone whether they know of reasons for having one. Other people may entertain the worst opinion of us in consequence of what we do, and may despise us as much as they like; so long as no one dares to give expression to his opinion, our honour remains untarnished. So if our actions and qualities compel the highest respect from other people, and they have no option but to give this respect,—as soon as anyone, no matter how wicked or foolish he may be, utters something depreciatory of us, our honour is offended, nay, gone for ever, unless we can manage to restore it. A superfluous proof of what I say, namely, that knightly honour depends, not upon what people think, but upon what they say, is furnished by the fact that insults can be withdrawn, or, if necessary, form the subject of an apology, which makes them as though they had never been uttered. Whether the opinion which underlay the expression has also been rectified, and why the expression should ever have been used, are questions which are perfectly unimportant: so long as the statement is withdrawn, all is well. The truth is that conduct of this kind aims, not at earning respect, but at extorting it.

(2.) In the second place, this sort of honour rests, not on what a man does, but on what he suffers, the obstacles he encounters; differing from the honour which prevails in all else, in consisting, not in what he says or does himself, but in what another man says or does. His honour is thus at the mercy of every man who can talk it away on the tip of his tongue; and if he attacks it, in a moment it is gone for ever,— unless the man who is attacked manages to wrest it back again by a process which I shall mention presently, a process which involves danger to his life, health, freedom, property and peace of mind. A man's whole conduct may be in accordance with the most righteous and noble principles, his spirit may be the purest that ever breathed, his intellect of the very highest order; and yet his honour may disappear the moment that anyone is pleased to insult him, anyone at all who has not offended against this code of honour himself, let him be the most worthless rascal or the most stupid beast, an idler, gambler, debtor, a man, in short, of no account at all. It is usually this sort of fellow who likes to insult people; for, as Seneca[1] rightly remarks, *ut quisque contemtissimus et ludibrio est, ita solutissimœ linguœ est*—the more contemptible and ridiculous a man is, the readier he is with his tongue. His insults are most likely to be directed against the very kind of man I have described, because people of different tastes can never be friends, and the sight of pre-eminent merit is apt to raise the secret ire of a ne'er-do-well. What Goethe says in the *Westöstlicher Divan* is quite true, that it is useless to complain against your enemies; for they can never become your friends, if your whole being is a standing reproach to them:—

> Was klagst du über Feinde?
> Sollten Solche je werden Freunde
> Denen das Wesen, wie du bist,
> Im stillen ein ewiger Vorwurf ist?

It is obvious that people of this worthless description have good cause to be thankful to the principle of honour, because it puts them on a level with people who in every other respect stand far above them. If a fellow likes to insult any one, attribute to him, for example, some bad quality, this is taken *prima facie* as a well-founded opinion, true in fact; a decree, as it were, with all the force of law; nay, if it is not at once wiped out in blood, it is a judgment which holds good and valid to all time. In other words, the man who is insulted remains—in the eyes of all *honourable people*—what the man who uttered the insult—even

---

[1]*De Constantia*, 11.

though he were the greatest wretch on earth—was pleased to call him;
for he has *put up with* the insult—the technical term, I believe.
Accordingly, all *honourable people* will have nothing more to do with
him, and treat him like a leper, and, it may be, refuse to go into any
company where he may be found, and so on.

This wise proceeding may, I think, be traced back to the fact that in
the Middle Age, up to the fifteenth century, it was not the accuser in
any criminal process who had to prove the guilt of the accused, but the
accused who had to prove his innocence.[1] This he could do by swear-
ing he was not guilty; and his backers—*consacramentales*—had to
come and swear that in their opinion he was incapable of perjury. If he
could find no one to help him in this way, or the accuser took objec-
tion to his backers, recourse was had to trial by *the Judgment of God*,
which generally meant a duel. For the accused was now *in disgrace*,[2]
and had to clear himself. Here, then, is the origin of the notion of disgrace, and of that whole system which prevails now-a-days amongst
honourable people,—only that the oath is omitted. This is also the explanation of that deep feeling of indignation which *honourable people*
are called upon to show if they are given the lie; it is a reproach which
they say must be wiped out in blood. It seldom comes to this pass, however, though lies are of common occurrence; but in England, more
than elsewhere, it is a superstition which has taken very deep root. As a
matter of order, a man who threatens to kill another for telling a lie
should never have told one himself. The fact is, that the criminal trial
of the Middle Age also admitted of a shorter form. In reply to the
charge, the accused answered: *That is a lie*; whereupon it was left to be
decided by *the Judgment of God*. Hence, the code of knightly honour
prescribes that, when the lie is given, an appeal to arms follows as a
matter of course. So much, then, for the theory of insult.

But there is something even worse than insult, something so dreadful that I must beg pardon of all *honourable people* for so much as mentioning it in this code of knightly honour; for I know they will shiver,
and their hair will stand on end, at the very thought of it—the *summum
malum*, the greatest evil on earth, worse than death and damnation. A
man may give another—*horribile dictu!*—a slap or a blow. This is such
an awful thing, and so utterly fatal to all honour, that, while any other
species of insult may be healed by blood-letting, this can be cured only
by the *coup-de-grâce*.

---

[1] See C. G. von Wächter's *Beiträge zur deutschen Geschichte*, especially the chapter on
criminal law.

[2] *Translator's Note.* It is true that this expression has another and special meaning in the
technical terminology of Chivalry, but it is the nearest English equivalent which I can
find for the German—*ein Bescholtener*.

(3.) In the third place, this kind of honour has absolutely nothing to do with what a man may be in and for himself; or, again, with the question whether his moral character can ever become better or worse, and all such pedantic inquiries. If your honour happens to be attacked, or to all appearances gone, it can very soon be restored in its entirety if you are only quick enough in having recourse to the one universal remedy—*a duel*. But if the aggressor does not belong to the classes which recognise the code of knightly honour, or has himself once offended against it, there is a safer way of meeting any attack upon your honour, whether it consists in blows, or merely in words. If you are armed, you can strike down your opponent on the spot, or perhaps an hour later. This will restore your honour.

But if you wish to avoid such an extreme step, from fear of any unpleasant consequences arising therefrom, or from uncertainty as to whether the aggressor is subject to the laws of knightly honour or not, there is another means of making your position good, namely, the *Avantage*. This consists in returning rudeness with still greater rudeness; and if insults are no use, you can try a blow, which forms a sort of climax in the redemption of your honour; for instance, a box on the ear may be cured by a blow with a stick, and a blow with a stick by a thrashing with a horsewhip; and, as the approved remedy for this last, some people recommend you to spit at your opponent.[1] If all these means are of no avail, you must not shrink from drawing blood. And the reason for these methods of wiping out insult is, in this code, as follows:

(4.) To receive an insult is disgraceful; to give one, honourable. Let me take an example. My opponent has truth, right and reason on his side. Very well. I insult him. Thereupon right and honour leave him and come to me, and, for the time being, he has lost them—until he gets them back, not by the exercise of right or reason, but by shooting and sticking me. Accordingly, rudeness is a quality which, in point of honour, is a substitute for any other and outweighs them all. The rudest is always right. What more do you want? However stupid, bad or wicked a man may have been, if he is only rude into the bargain, he condones and legitimises all his faults. If in any discussion or conversation, another man shows more knowledge, greater love of truth, a sounder judgment, better understanding than we, or generally exhibits intellectual qualities which cast ours into the shade, we can at once annul his superiority and our own shallowness, and in our turn be superior to him, by being insulting and offensive. For rudeness is better

---

[1] *Translator's Note.* It must be remembered that Schopenhauer is here describing, or perhaps caricaturing, the manners and customs of the German aristocracy of half a century ago. Now, of course, *nous avons changé tout cela!*

than any argument; it totally eclipses intellect. If our opponent does not care for our mode of attack, and will not answer still more rudely, so as to plunge us into the ignoble rivalry of the *Avantage*, we are the victors and honour is on our side. Truth, knowledge, understanding, intellect, wit, must beat a retreat and leave the field to this almighty insolence.

Honourable people immediately make a show of mounting their warhorse, if anyone utters an opinion adverse to theirs, or shows more intelligence than they can muster; and if in any controversy they are at a loss for a reply, they look about for some weapon of rudeness, which will serve as well and come readier to hand; so they retire masters of the position. It must now be obvious that people are quite right in applauding this principle of honour as having ennobled the tone of society. This principle springs from another, which forms the heart and soul of the entire code.

(5.) Fifthly, the code implies that the highest court to which a man can appeal in any differences he may have with another on a point of honour is the court of physical force, that is, of brutality. Every piece of rudeness is, strictly speaking, an appeal to brutality; for it is a declaration that intellectual strength and moral insight are incompetent to decide, and that the battle must be fought out by physical force—a struggle which, in the case of man, whom Franklin defines as *a toolmaking animal*, is decided by the weapons peculiar to the species; and the decision is irrevocable. This is the well-known principle of *the right of might*—irony, of course, like *the wit of a fool*, a parallel phrase. The honour of a knight may be called the glory of might.

(6.) Lastly, if, as we saw above, civic honour is very scrupulous in the matter of *meum* and *tuum*, paying great respect to obligations and a promise once made, the code we are here discussing displays, on the other hand, the noblest liberality. There is only one word which may not be broken, *the word of honour*—upon my *honour*, as people say—the presumption being, of course, that every other form of promise may be broken. Nay, if the worst comes to the worst, it is easy to break even one's word of honour, and still remain honourable—again by adopting that universal remedy, the duel, and fighting with those who maintain that we pledged our word. Further, there is one debt, and one alone, that under no circumstances must be left unpaid—a gambling debt, which has accordingly been called *a debt of honour*. In all other kinds of debt you may cheat Jews and Christians are much as you like; and your knightly honour remains without a stain.

The unprejudiced reader will see at once that such a strange, savage and ridiculous code of honour as this has no foundation in human nature, nor any warrant in a healthy view of human affairs. The extremely narrow sphere of its operation serves only to intensify the feeling, which is exclusively confined to Europe since the Middle Age, and then only to the upper classes, officers and soldiers, and people who imitate them. Neither Greeks nor Romans knew anything of this code of honour or of its principles; nor the highly civilised nations of Asia, ancient or modern. Amongst them no other kind of honour is recognised but that which I discussed first, in virtue of which a man is what he shows himself to be by his actions, not what any wagging tongue is pleased to say of him. They thought that what a man said or did might perhaps affect his own honour, but not any other man's. To them, a blow was but a blow—and any horse or donkey could give a harder one—a blow which under certain circumstances might make a man angry and demand immediate vengeance; but it had nothing to do with honour. No one kept account of blows or insulting words, or of the *satisfaction* which was demanded or omitted to be demanded. Yet in personal bravery and contempt of death, the ancients were certainly not inferior to the nations of Christian Europe. The Greeks and Romans were thorough heroes, if you like; but they knew nothing about *point d'honneur*. If they had any idea of a duel, it was totally unconnected with the life of the nobles; it was merely the exhibition of mercenary gladiators, slaves devoted to slaughter, condemned criminals, who, alternately with wild beasts, were set to butcher one another to make a Roman holiday. When Christianity was introduced, gladiatorial shows were done away with, and their place taken, in Christian times, by the duel, which was a way of settling difficulties by *the Judgment of God*. If the gladiatorial fight was a cruel sacrifice to the prevailing desire for great spectacles, duelling is a cruel sacrifice to existing prejudices—a sacrifice, not of criminals, slaves and prisoners, but of the noble and the free.[1]

There are a great many traits in the character of the ancients which show that they were entirely free from these prejudices. When, for instance, Marius was summoned to a duel by a Teutonic chief, he returned answer to the effect that, if the chief were tired of his life, he might go and hang himself; at the same time he offered him a veteran gladiator for a round or two. Plutarch relates in his life of Themistocles that Eurybiades, who was in command of the fleet, once raised his stick to strike him; whereupon Themistocles, instead of drawing his sword, simply said: *Strike, but hear me*. How sorry the reader must be, if he is an *honourable* man, to find that we have no information that the Athenian officers refused in a body to serve any longer under Themis-

---

[1]*Translator's Note.* These and other remarks on duelling will no doubt wear a belated look to English readers; but they are hardly yet antiquated for most parts of the Continent.

tocles, if he acted like that! There is a modern French writer who declares that if anyone considers Demosthenes a man of honour, his ignorance will excite a smile of pity; and that Cicero was not a man of
honour either![1] In a certain passage in Plato's *Laws*,[2] the philosopher
speaks at length of αἰκία or *assault*, showing us clearly enough that the
ancients had no notion of any feeling of honour in connection with
such matters. Socrates' frequent discussions were often followed by his
being severely handled, and he bore it all mildly. Once, for instance,
when somebody kicked him, the patience with which he took the insult surprised one of his friends. *Do you think*, said Socrates, *that if an
ass happened to kick me, I should resent it?*[3] On another occasion, when
he was asked, *Has not that fellow abused and insulted you? No*, was his
answer, *what he says is not addressed to me.*[4] Stobæus has preserved a
long passage from Musonius, from which we can see how the ancients
treated insults. They knew no other form of satisfaction than that which
the law provided, and wise people despised even this. If a Greek received a box on the ear, he could get satisfaction by the aid of the law;
as is evident from Plato's *Gorgias*, where Socrates' opinion may be
found. The same thing may be seen in the account given by Gellius of
one Lucius Veratius, who had the audacity to give some Roman citizens whom he met on the road a box on the ear, without any provoca-
tion whatever; but to avoid any ulterior consequences, he told a slave
to bring a bag of small money, and on the spot paid the trivial legal
penalty to the men whom he had astonished by his conduct.

Crates, the celebrated Cynic philosopher, got such a box on the ear
from Nicodromus, the musician, that his face swelled up and became
black and blue; whereupon he put a label on his forehead, with the in-
scription, *Nicodromus fecit*, which brought much disgrace to the
fluteplayer who had committed such a piece of brutality upon the man
whom all Athens honoured as a household god.[5] And in a letter to
Melesippus, Diogenes of Sinope tells us that he got a beating from the
drunken sons of the Athenians; but he adds that it was a matter of no
importance.[6] And Seneca devotes the last few chapters of his *De
Constantia* to a lengthy discussion on insult—*contumelia*; in order to
show that a wise man will take no notice of it. In Chapter XIV he says,
What shall a wise man do, if he is given a blow? What Cato did, when

---

[1]*Soirées littéraires*: par C. Durand. Rouen, 1828.
[2]Bk. IX.
[3]Diogenes Laertius, ii., 21.
[4]*Ibid* 36.
[5]Diogenes Laertius, vi. 87, and Apul: Flor: p. 126.
[6]Cf. Casaubon's Note, ad Diog. Laert., vi. 33.

some one struck him on the mouth;—*not fire up or avenge the insult, or even return the blow, but simply ignore it.*

Yes, you say, *but these men were philosophers.*—And you are fools, eh? Precisely.

It is clear that the whole code of knightly honour was utterly unknown to the ancients; for the simple reason that they always took a natural and unprejudiced view of human affairs, and did not allow themselves to be influenced by any such vicious and abominable folly. A blow in the face was to them a blow and nothing more, a trivial physical injury; whereas the moderns make a catastrophe out of it, a theme for a tragedy; as, for instance, in the *Cid* of Corneille, or in a recent German comedy of middle-class life, called *The Power of Circumstance*, which should have been entitled *The Power of Prejudice*. If a member of the National Assembly at Paris got a blow on the ear, it would resound from one end of Europe to the other. The examples which I have given of the way in which such an occurrence would have been treated in classic times may not suit the ideas of *honourable people*; so let me recommend to their notice, as a kind of antidote, the story of Monsieur Desglands in Diderot's masterpiece, *Jacques le fataliste*. It is an excellent specimen of modern knightly honour, which, no doubt, they will find enjoyable and edifying.[1]

From what I have said it must be quite evident that the principle of knightly honour has no essential and spontaneous origin in human nature. It is an artificial product, and its source is not hard to find. Its existence obviously dates from the time when people used their fists more than their heads, when priestcraft had enchained the human intellect, the much bepraised Middle Age, with its system of chivalry. That was the time when people let the Almighty not only care for them but judge for them too; when difficult cases were decided by an ordeal, a *Judgment of God*; which, with few exceptions, meant a duel, not only where nobles were concerned, but in the case of ordinary citizens as

---

[1]*Translator's Note.* The story to which Schopenhauer here refers is briefly as follows: Two gentlemen, one of whom was named Desglands, were paying court to the same lady. As they sat at table side by side, with the lady opposite, Desglands did his best to charm her with his conversation; but she pretended not to hear him, and kept looking at his rival. In the agony of jealousy, Desglands, as he was holding a fresh egg in his hand, involuntarily crushed it; the shell broke, and its contents bespattered his rival's face. Seeing him raise his hand, Desglands seized it and whispered: *Sir, I take it as given.* The next day Desglands appeared with a large piece of black sticking-plaster upon his right cheek. In the duel which followed, Desglands severely wounded his rival; upon which he reduced the size of the plaster. When his rival recovered, they had another duel; Desglands drew blood again, and again made his plaster a little smaller; and so on for five or six times. After every duel Desglands' plaster grew less and less, until at last his rival was killed.

well. There is a neat illustration of this in Shakespeare's Henry VI.[1] Every judicial sentence was subject to an appeal to arms—a court, as it were, of higher instance, namely, *the Judgment of God:* and this really meant that physical strength and activity, that is, our animal nature, usurped the place of reason on the judgment seat, deciding in matters of right and wrong, not by what a man had done, but by the force with which he was opposed, the same system, in fact, as prevails to-day under the principles of knightly honour. If any one doubts that such is really the origin of our modern duel, let him read an excellent work by J. B. Millingen, *The History of Duelling.*[2] Nay, you may still find amongst the supporters of the system,—who, by the way, are not usually the most educated or thoughtful of men,—some who look upon the result of a duel as really constituting a divine judgment in the matter in dispute; no doubt in consequence of the traditional feeling on the subject.

But leaving aside the question of origin, it must now be clear to us that the main tendency of the principle is to use physical menace for the purpose of extorting an appearance of respect which is deemed too difficult or superfluous to acquire in reality; a proceeding which comes to much the same thing as if you were to prove the warmth of your room by holding your hand on the thermometer and so make it rise. In fact, the kernel of the matter is this: whereas civic honour aims at peaceable intercourse, and consists in the opinion of other people that *we deserve full confidence,* because we pay unconditional respect to their rights, knightly honour, on the other hand, lays down that *we are to be feared,* as being determined at all costs to maintain our own.

As not much reliance can be placed upon human integrity, the principle that it is more essential to arouse fear than to invite confidence would not, perhaps, be a false one, if we were living in a state of nature, where every man would have to protect himself and directly maintain his own rights. But in civilised life, where the State undertakes the protection of our person and property, the principle is no longer applicable: it stands, like the castles and watch-towers of the age when might was right, a useless and forlorn object, amidst well-tilled fields and frequented roads, or even railways.

Accordingly, the application of knightly honour, which still recognises this principle, is confined to those small cases of personal assault which meet with but slight punishment at the hands of the law, or even none at all, for *de minimis non,*—mere trivial wrongs, committed sometimes only in jest. The consequence of this limited application of the

---

[1]Part II., Act 2, Sc. 3.
[2]Published in 1849.

principle is that it has forced itself into an exaggerated respect for the value of the person,—a respect utterly alien to the nature, constitution or destiny of man—which it has elevated into a species of sanctity: and as it considers that the State has imposed a very insufficient penalty on the commission of such trivial injuries, it takes upon itself to punish them by attacking the aggressor in life or limb. The whole thing manifestly rests upon an excessive degree of arrogant pride, which, completely forgetting what man really is, claims that he shall be absolutely free from all attack or even censure. Those who determine to carry out this principle by main force, and announce, as their rule of action, *whoever insults or strikes me shall die!* ought for their pains to be banished the country.[1]

As a palliative to this rash arrogance, people are in the habit of giving way on everything. If two intrepid persons meet, and neither will give way, the slightest difference may cause a shower of abuse, then fisticuffs, and, finally, a fatal blow; so that it would really be a more decorous proceeding to omit the intermediate steps and appeal to arms at once. An appeal to arms has its own special formalities; and these have developed into a rigid and precise system of laws and regulations, together forming the most solemn farce there is,—a regular temple of honour dedicated to folly! For if two intrepid persons dispute over some trivial matter, (more important affairs are dealt with by law), one of them, the cleverer of the two, will of course yield; and they will agree to differ. That this is so is proved by the fact that common people,—or, rather, the numerous classes of the community who do not acknowledge the principle of knightly honour, let any dispute run its natural course. Amongst these classes homicide is a hundredfold rarer than among those—and they amount, perhaps, in all, to hardly one in a

---

[1] Knightly honour is the child of pride and folly, and it is *need*, not pride, which is the heritage of the human race. It is a very remarkable fact that this extreme form of pride should be found exclusively amongst the adherents of the religion which teaches the deepest humility. Still, this pride must not be put down to religion, but, rather, to the feudal system, which made every nobleman a petty sovereign who recognised no human judge, and learned to regard his person as sacred and inviolable, and any attack upon it, or any blow or insulting word, as an offence punishable by death. The principle of knightly honour and of the duel was at first confined to the nobles, and, later on, also to officers in the army, who, enjoying a kind of off-and-on relationship with the upper classes, though they were never incorporated with them, were anxious not to be behind them. It is true that duels were the product of the old ordeals; but the latter are not the foundation, but rather the consequence and application of the principle of honour: the man who recognised no human judge appealed to the divine. Ordeals, however, are not peculiar to Christendom: they may be found in great force among the Hindoos, especially of ancient times; and there are traces of them even now.

thousand,—who pay homage to the principle: and even blows are of no very frequent occurrence.

Then it has been said that the manners and tone of good society are ultimately based upon this principle of honour, which, with its system of duels, is made out to be a bulwark against the assaults of savagery and rudeness. But Athens, Corinth and Rome could assuredly boast of good, nay, excellent society, and manners and tone of a high order, without any support from the bogey of knightly honour. It is true that women did not occupy that prominent place in ancient society which they hold now, when conversation has taken on a frivolous and trifling character, to the exclusion of that weighty discourse which distinguished the ancients. This change has certainly contributed a great deal to bring about the tendency, which is observable in good society now-a-days, to prefer personal courage to the possession of any other quality. The fact is that personal courage is really a very subordinate virtue,—merely the distinguishing mark of a subaltern,—a virtue, indeed, in which we are surpassed by the lower animals; or else you would not hear people say, *as brave as a lion*. Far from being the pillar of society, knightly honour affords a sure asylum, in general for dishonesty and wickedness, and also for small incivilities, want of consideration and unmannerliness. Rude behaviour is often passed over in silence because no one cares to risk his neck in correcting it.

After what I have said, it will not appear strange that the duelling system is carried to the highest pitch of sanguinary zeal precisely in that nation whose political and financial records show that they are not too honourable. What that nation is like in its private and domestic life, is a question which may be best put to those who are experienced in the matter. Their urbanity and social culture have long been conspicuous by their absence.

There is no truth, then, in such pretexts. It can be urged with more justice that as, when you snarl at a dog, he snarls in return, and when you pet him, he fawns; so it lies in the nature of men to return hostility by hostility, and to be embittered and irritated at any signs of depreciatory treatment or hatred, and, as Cicero says, *there is something so penetrating in the shaft of envy that even men of wisdom and worth find its wound a painful one*; and nowhere in the world, except, perhaps, in a few religious sects, is an insult or a blow taken with equanimity. And yet a natural view of either would in no case demand anything more than a requital proportionate to the offence, and would never go the length of assigning *death* as the proper penalty for anyone who accuses another of lying or stupidity or cowardice. The old German theory of *blood for a blow* is a revolting superstition of the age of chivalry. And in any case the return or requital of an insult is dictated by anger, and not by any such obligation of honour and duty as the advocates of chivalry seek to attach to it. The fact is that, the greater the truth, the greater the slander; and it is clear that the slightest hint of some real delinquency will give much greater offence than a most terrible accusation which is perfectly baseless: so that a man who is quite sure that he has done nothing to deserve a reproach may treat it with contempt, and will be safe in doing so. The theory of honour demands that he shall show a susceptibility which he does not possess, and take bloody vengeance for insults which he cannot feel. A man must himself have but a poor opinion of his own worth who hastens to prevent the utterance of an unfavourable opinion by giving his enemy a black eye.

True appreciation of his own value will make a man really indifferent to insult; but if he cannot help resenting it, a little shrewdness and culture will enable him to save appearances and dissemble his anger. If we could only get rid of this superstition about honour—the idea, I mean, that it disappears when you are insulted, and can be restored by returning the insult; if we could only stop people from thinking that wrong, brutality and insolence can be legalised by expressing readiness to give satisfaction, that is, to fight in defence of it, we should all soon come to the general opinion that insult and depreciation are like a battle in which the loser wins; and that, as Vincenzo Monti says, abuse resembles a church-procession, because it always returns to the point from which it set out. If we could only get people to look upon insult in this light, we should no longer have to say something rude in order to prove that we are in the right. Now, unfortunately, if we want to take a serious view of any question, we have first of all to consider whether it will not give offence in some way or other to the dullard, who generally shows alarm and resentment at the merest sign of intelligence: and it may easily happen that the head which contains the intelligent view has to be pitted against the noddle which is empty of everything but narrowness and stupidity. If all this were done away with, intellectual superiority could take the leading place in society which is its due—a place now occupied, though people do not like to confess it, by excellence of physique, mere fighting pluck, in fact; and the natural effect of such a change would be that the best kind of people would have one reason the less for withdrawing from society. This would pave the way for the introduction of real courtesy and genuinely good society, such as undoubtedly existed in Athens, Corinth and Rome. If anyone wants to see a good example of what I mean, I should like him to read Xenophon's *Banquet*.

The last argument in defence of knightly honour no doubt is, that, but for its existence, the world—awful thought!—would be a regular bear-garden. To which I may briefly reply that nine hundred and ninety-nine people out of a thousand who do not recognise the code, have often given and received a blow without any fatal consequences; whereas amongst the adherents of the code a blow usually means death to one of the parties. But let me examine this argument more closely.

I have often tried to find some tenable or, at any rate, plausible basis—other than a merely conventional one—some positive reasons, that is to say, for the rooted conviction which a portion of mankind entertains, that a blow is a very dreadful thing; but I have looked for it in vain, either in the animal or in the rational side of human nature. A blow is, and always will be, a trivial physical injury which one man can do to another; proving, thereby, nothing more than his superiority in strength or skill, or that his enemy was off his guard. Analysis will carry us no further. The same knight who regards a blow from the human hand as the greatest of evils, if he gets a ten times harder blow from his horse, will give you the assurance, as he limps away in suppressed pain, that it is a matter of no consequence whatever. So I have come to think that it is the human hand which is at the bottom of the mischief. And yet in a battle the knight may get cuts and thrusts from the same hand, and still assure you that his wounds are not worth mentioning. Now, I hear that a blow from the flat of a sword is not by any means so bad as a blow with a stick; and that, a short time ago, cadets were liable to be punished by the one but not the other, and that the very greatest honour of all is the *accolade*. This is all the psychological or moral basis that I can find; and so there is nothing left me but to pronounce the whole thing an antiquated superstition that has taken deep root, and one more of the many examples which show the force of tradition. My view is confirmed by the well-known fact that in China a beating with a bamboo is a very frequent punishment for the common people, and even for officials of every class, which shows that human nature, even in a highly civilised state, does not run in the same groove here and in China.

On the contrary, an unprejudiced view of human nature shows that it is just as natural for man to beat as it is for savage animals to bite and rend in pieces, or for horned beasts to butt or push. Man may be said to be the animal that beats. Hence it is revolting to our sense of the fitness of things to hear, as we sometimes do, that one man has bitten another; on the other hand, it is a natural and everyday occurrence for him to get blows or give them. It is intelligible enough that, as we become educated, we are glad to dispense with blows by a system of mutual restraint. But it is a cruel thing to compel a nation or a single class to regard a blow as an awful misfortune which must have death and murder for its consequences. There are too many genuine evils in the world to allow of our increasing them by imaginary misfortunes, which bring real ones in their train; and yet this is the precise effect of the superstition, which thus proves itself at once stupid and malign.

It does not seem to me wise of governments and legislative bodies to promote any such folly by attempting to do away with flogging as a punishment in civil or military life. Their idea is that they are acting in the interests of humanity; but, in point of fact, they are doing just the opposite; for the abolition of flogging will serve only to strengthen this inhuman and abominable superstition, to which so many sacrifices have already been made. For all offences, except the worst, a beating is the obvious and therefore the natural penalty; and a man who will not listen to reason will yield to blows. It seems to me right and proper to administer corporal punishment to the man who possesses nothing and therefore cannot be fined, or cannot be put in prison because his master's interests would suffer by the loss of his services. There are really no arguments against it; only mere talk about *the dignity of man*—talk which proceeds, not from any clear notions on the subject, but from the pernicious superstition I have been describing. That it is a superstition which lies at the bottom of the whole business is proved by an almost laughable example. Not long ago, in the military discipline of many countries, the cat was replaced by the stick. In either case the object was to produce physical pain; but the latter method involved no disgrace, and was not derogatory to honour.

By promoting this superstition, the State is playing into the hands of the principle of knightly honour, and therefore of the duel; while at the same time it is trying, or at any rate it pretends that it is trying, to abolish the duel by legislative enactment. As a natural consequence we find that this fragment of the theory that *might is right*, which has come down to us from the most savage days of the Middle Age, has still in this nineteenth century a good deal of life left in it—more shame to us! It is high time for the principle to be driven out bag and baggage. Now-a-days, no one is allowed to set dogs or cocks to fight each other,—at any rate, in England it is a penal offence,—but men are plunged into deadly strife, against their will, by the operation of this ridiculous, superstitious and absurd principle, which imposes upon us the obligation, as its narrow-minded supporters and advocates declare, of fighting with one another like gladiators, for any little trifle. Let me recommend our purists to adopt the expression *baiting*,[1] instead of *duel*, which probably comes to us, not from the Latin *duellum*, but from the Spanish *duelo*,—meaning suffering, nuisance, annoyance.

In any case, we may well laugh at the pedantic excess to which this foolish system has been carried. It is really revolting that this principle,

[1] *Ritterhetze.*

with its absurd code, can form a power within the State—*imperium in imperio*—a power too easily put in motion, which, recognising no right but might, tyrannises over the classes which come within its range, by keeping up a sort of inquisition, before which any one may be haled on the most flimsy pretext, and there and then be tried on an issue of life and death between himself and his opponent. This is the lurking place from which every rascal, if he only belongs to the classes in question, may menace and even exterminate the noblest and best of men, who, as such, must of course be an object of hatred to him. Our system of justice and police-protection has made it impossible in these days for any scoundrel in the street to attack us with—*Your money or your life!* and common sense ought now to be able to prevent rogues disturbing the peaceable intercourse of society by coming at us with—*Your honour or your life!* An end should be put to the burden which weighs upon the higher classes—the burden, I mean, of having to be ready every moment to expose life and limb to the mercy of any-one who takes it into his rascally head to be coarse, rude, foolish or malicious. It is perfectly atrocious that a pair of silly, passionate boys should be wounded, maimed or even killed, simply because they have had a few words.

The strength of this tyrannical power within the State, and the force of the superstition, may be measured by the fact that people who are prevented from restoring their knightly honour by the superior or infe-rior rank of their aggressor, or anything else that puts the persons on a different level, often come to a tragic-comic end by committing suicide in sheer despair. You may generally know a thing to be false and ridicu-lous by finding that, if it is carried to its logical conclusion, it results in a contradiction; and here, too, we have a very glaring absurdity. For an officer is forbidden to take part in a duel; but if he is challenged and declines to come out, he is punished by being dismissed the service.

As I am on the matter, let me be more frank still. The important dis-tinction, which is often insisted upon, between killing your enemy in a fair fight with equal weapons, and lying in ambush for him, is entirely a corollary of the fact that the power within the State, of which I have spoken, recognises no other right than might, that is, the right of the stronger, and appeals to a *Judgment of God* as the basis of the whole code. For to kill a man in a fair fight, is to prove that you are superior to him in strength or skill; and to justify the deed, *you must assume that the right of the stronger is really a right.*

But the truth is that, if my opponent is unable to defend himself, it gives me the possibility, but not by any means the right, of killing him. The *right*, the *moral justification*, must depend entirely upon the *mo-tives* which I have for taking his life. Even supposing that I have sufficient motive for taking a man's life, there is no reason why I should make his death depend upon whether I can shoot or fence better than he. In such a case, it is immaterial in what way I kill him, whether I attack him from the front or the rear. From a moral point of view, the right of the stronger is no more convincing than the right of the more skillful; and it is skill which is employed if you murder a man treacherously. Might and skill are in this case equally right: in a duel, for instance, both the one and the other come into play; for a feint is only another name for treachery. If I consider myself morally justified in taking a man's life, it is stupid of me to try first of all whether he can shoot or fence better than I; as, if he can, he will not only have wronged me, but have taken my life into the bargain.

It is Rousseau's opinion that the proper way to avenge an insult is, not to fight a duel with your aggressor, but to assassinate him,—an opinion, however, which he is cautious enough only just to indicate in a mysterious note to one of the books of his *Emile*. This shows the philosopher so completely under the influence of the mediæval superstition of knightly honour that he considers it justifiable to murder a man who accuses you of lying; whilst he must have known that every man, and himself especially, has deserved to have the lie given him times without number.

The prejudice which justifies the killing of your adversary, so long as it is done in an open contest and with equal weapons, obviously looks upon might as really right, and a duel as the interference of God. The Italian who, in a fit of rage, falls upon his aggressor wherever he finds him, and despatches him without any ceremony, acts, at any rate, consistently and naturally: he may be cleverer, but he is not worse, than the duellist. If you say, I am justified in killing my adversary in a duel, because he is at the moment doing his best to kill me, I can reply that it is your challenge which has placed him under the necessity of defending himself; and that by mutually putting it on the ground of self-defence, the combatants are seeking a plausible pretext for committing murder. I should rather justify the deed by the legal maxim *Volenti non fit injuria*; because the parties mutually agree to set their life upon the issue. This argument may, however, be rebutted by showing that the injured party is not injured *volens*; because it is this tyrannical principle of knightly honour, with its absurd code, which forcibly drags one at least of the combatants before a bloody inquisition.

I have been rather prolix on the subject of knightly honour, but I had good reasons for being so, because the Augean stable of moral and intellectual enormity in this world can be cleaned out only with the besom of philosophy. There are two things which more than all else

serve to make the social arrangements of modern life compare un-
favourably with those of antiquity, by giving our age a gloomy, dark and
sinister aspect, from which antiquity, fresh, natural and, as it were, in
the morning of life, is completely free; I mean modern honour and
modern disease,—*par nobile fratrum!*—which have combined to poi-
son all the relations of life, whether public or private. The second of
this noble pair extends its influence much farther than at first appears
to be the case, as being not merely a physical, but also a moral disease.
From the time that poisoned arrows have been found in Cupid's
quiver, an estranging, hostile, nay, devilish element has entered into
the relations of men and women, like a sinister thread of fear and mis-
trust in the warp and woof of their intercourse; indirectly shaking the
foundations of human fellowship, and so more or less affecting the
whole tenor of existence. But it would be beside my present purpose to
pursue the subject further.

An influence analogous to this, though working on other lines, is ex-
erted by the principle of knightly honour,—that solemn farce, unknown to the ancient world, which makes modern society stiff, gloomy
and timid, forcing us to keep the strictest watch on every word that falls.
Nor is this all. The principle is a universal Minotaur; and the goodly
company of the sons of noble houses which it demands in yearly trib-
ute, comes, not from one country alone, as of old, but from every land
in Europe. It is high time to make a regular attack upon this foolish system; and this is what I am trying to do now. Would that these two mon-
sters of the modern world might disappear before the end of the
century!

Let us hope that medicine may be able to find some means of pre-
venting the one, and that, by clearing our ideas, philosophy may put an
end to the other; for it is only by clearing our ideas that the evil can be
eradicated. Governments have tried to do so by legislation, and failed.

Still, if they are really concerned to suppress the duelling system;
and if the small success that has attended their efforts is really due only
to their inability to cope with the evil, I do not mind proposing a law
the success of which I am prepared to guarantee. It will involve no sanguinary measures, and can be put into operation without recourse either to the scaffold or the gallows, or to imprisonment for life. It is a
small homœopathic pilule, with no serious after-effects. If any man
send or accept a challenge, let the corporal take him before the guard
house, and there give him, in broad daylight, twelve strokes with a stick
à la Chinoise; a non-commissioned officer or a private to receive six. If
a duel has actually taken place, the usual criminal proceedings should
be instituted.

A person with knightly notions might, perhaps, object that, if such a punishment were carried out, a man of honour would possibly shoot himself; to which I should answer that it is better for a fool like that to shoot himself rather than other people. However, I know very well that governments are not really in earnest about putting down duelling. Civil officials, and much more so, officers in the army, (except those in the highest positions), are paid most inadequately for the services they perform; and the deficiency is made up by honour, which is represented by titles and orders, and, in general, by the system of rank and distinction. The duel is, so to speak, a very serviceable extra-horse for people of rank: so they are trained in the knowledge of it at the universities. The accidents which happen to those who use it make up in blood for the deficiency of the pay.

Just to complete the discussion, let me here mention the subject of *national honour*. It is the honour of a nation as a unit in the aggregate of nations. And as there is no court to appeal to but the court of force; and as every nation must be prepared to defend its own interests, the honour of a nation consists in establishing the opinion, not only that it may be trusted (its credit), but also that it is to be feared. An attack upon its rights must never be allowed to pass unheeded. It is a combination of civic and of knightly honour.

Section 5.—Fame.

Under the heading of place in the estimation of the world we have put *Fame*; and this we must now proceed to consider.

Fame and honour are twins; and twins, too, like Castor and Pollux, of whom the one was mortal and the other was not. Fame is the undying brother of ephemeral honour. I speak, of course, of the highest kind of fame, that is, of fame in the true and genuine sense of the word; for, to be sure, there are many sorts of fame, some of which last but a day. Honour is concerned merely with such qualities as everyone may be expected to show under similar circumstances; fame only with those which cannot be required of any man. Honour is of qualities which everyone has a right to attribute to himself; fame only of those which should be left to others to attribute. Whilst our honour extends as far as people have knowledge of us; fame runs in advance, and makes us known wherever it finds its way. Every one can make a claim to honour; very few to fame, as being attainable only in virtue of extraordinary achievements.

These achievements may be of two kinds, either *actions* or *works*; and so to fame there are two paths open. On the path of actions, a great heart is the chief recommendation; on that of works, a great head. Each of the two paths has its own peculiar advantages and detriments; and the chief difference between them is that actions are fleeting, while works remain. The influence of an action, be it never so noble, can last but a short time; but a work of genius is a living influence, beneficial and ennobling throughout the ages. All that can remain of actions is a memory, and that becomes weak and disfigured by time—a matter of indifference to us, until at last it is extinguished altogether; unless, indeed, history takes it up, and presents it, fossilized, to posterity. Works are immortal in themselves, and once committed to writing, may live for ever. Of Alexander the Great we have but the name and the record: but Plato and Aristotle, Homer and Horace are alive, and as directly at work to-day as they were in their own life-time. The *Vedas*, and their *Upanishads*, are still with us; but of all contemporaneous actions not a trace has come down to us.[1]

Another disadvantage under which actions labour is that they depend upon chance for the possibility of coming into existence; and hence, the fame they win does not flow entirely from their intrinsic value, but also from the circumstances which happened to lend them importance and lustre. Again, the fame of actions, if, as in war, they are purely personal, depends upon the testimony of fewer witnesses; and these are not always present, and even if present, are not always just or unbiassed observers. This disadvantage, however, is counterbalanced by the fact that actions have the advantage of being of a practical character, and, therefore, within the range of general human intelligence; so that when the facts have been correctly reported, justice is immediately done; unless, indeed, the motive underlying the action is not at first properly understood or appreciated. No action can be really understood apart from the motive which prompted it.

It is just the contrary with works. Their inception does not depend

---

[1]Accordingly it is a poor compliment, though sometimes a fashionable one, to try to pay honour to a work by calling it an action. For a work is something essentially higher in its nature. An action is always something based on motive, and, therefore, fragmentary and fleeting—a part, in fact, of that Will which is the universal and original element in the constitution of the world. But a great and beautiful work has a permanent character, as being of universal significance, and sprung from the Intellect, which rises, like a perfume, above the faults and follies of the world of Will.

The fame of a great action has this advantage, that it generally starts with a loud explosion, so loud, indeed, as to be heard all over Europe, whereas the fame of a great work is slow and gradual in its beginnings; the noise it makes is at first slight, but it goes on growing greater, until at last, after a hundred years perhaps, it attains its full force; but then it remains, because the works remain, for thousands of years. But in the other case, when the first explosion is over, the noise it makes grows less and less, and is heard by fewer and fewer persons; until it ends by the action having only a shadowy existence in the pages of history.

upon chance, but wholly and entirely upon their author; and whatever they are in and for themselves, that they remain as long as they live. Further, there is a difficulty in properly judging them, which becomes all the harder, the higher their character; often there are no persons competent to understand the work, and often no unbiassed or honest critics. Their fame, however, does not depend upon one judge only; they can enter an appeal to another. In the case of actions, as I have said, it is only their memory which comes down to posterity, and then only in the traditional form; but works are handed down themselves, and, except when parts of them have been lost, in the form in which they first appeared. In this case there is no room for any disfigurement of the facts; and any circumstances which may have prejudiced them in their origin, fall away with the lapse of time. Nay, it is often only after the lapse of time that the persons really competent to judge them appear—exceptional critics sitting in judgment on exceptional works, and giving their weighty verdicts in succession. These collectively form a perfectly just appreciation; and though there are cases where it has taken some hundreds of years to form it, no further lapse of time is able to reverse the verdict;—so secure and inevitable is the fame of a great work.

Whether authors ever live to see the dawn of their fame depends upon the chance of circumstance; and the higher and more important their works are, the less likelihood there is of their doing so. That was an incomparably fine saying of Seneca's, that fame follows merit as surely as the body casts a shadow; sometimes falling in front, and sometimes behind. And he goes on to remark that *though the envy of contemporaries be shown by universal silence, there will come those who will judge without enmity or favour.* From this remark it is manifest that even in Seneca's age there were rascals who understood the art of suppressing merit by maliciously ignoring its existence, and of concealing good work from the public in order to favour the bad. It is an art well understood in our day, too, manifesting itself, both then and now, in *an envious conspiracy of silence.*

As a general rule, the longer a man's fame is likely to last, the later it will be in coming; for all excellent products require time for their development. The fame which lasts to posterity is like an oak, of very slow growth; and that which endures but a little while, like plants which spring up in a year and then die; whilst false fame is like a fungus, shooting up in a night and perishing as soon.

And why? For this reason: the more a man belongs to posterity, in other words, to humanity in general, the more of an alien he is to his contemporaries; since his work is not meant for them as such, but only for them in so far as they form part of mankind at large; there is none of that familiar local colour about his productions which would appeal to them; and so what he does, fails of recognition because it is strange. People are more likely to appreciate the man who serves the circumstances of his own brief hour, or the temper of the moment,—belonging to it, and living and dying with it.

The general history of art and literature shows that the highest achievements of the human mind are, as a rule, not favourably received at first; but remain in obscurity until they win notice from intelligence of a higher order, by whose influence they are brought into a position which they then maintain, in virtue of the authority thus given them.

If the reason of this should be asked, it will be found that ultimately, a man can really understand and appreciate those things only which are of like nature with himself. The dull person will like what is dull, and the common person what is common; a man whose ideas are mixed will be attracted by confusion of thought; and folly will appeal to him who has no brains at all; but best of all, a man will like his own works, as being of a character thoroughly at one with himself. This is a truth as old as Epicharmus of fabulous memory—

> Θαυμαστὸν οὐδὲν ἐστί με ταῦθ' οὕτω λέγειν
> Καὶ ἀνδάνειν αὐτοῖσιν αὐτούς, καὶ δοκεῖν
> Καλῶς πεφυκέναι· καὶ γὰρ ὁ κύων κυνί
> Κάλλιστον εἶμεν φαίνεται, καὶ βοῦς βοΐ
> Ὄνος δ' ὄνῳ κάλλιστόν [ἐστιν], ὗς δ' ὑΐ.

The sense of this passage—for it should not be lost—is that we should not be surprised if people are pleased with themselves, and fancy that they are in good case; for to a dog the best thing in the world is a dog; to an ox, an ox; to an ass, an ass; and to a sow, a sow.

The strongest arm is unavailing to give impetus to a feather-weight; for, instead of speeding on its way and hitting its mark with effect, it will soon fall to the ground, having expended what little energy was given to it, and possessing no mass of its own to be the vehicle of momentum. So it is with great and noble thoughts, nay, with the very masterpieces of genius, when there are none but little, weak, and perverse minds to appreciate them,—a fact which has been deplored by a chorus of the wise in all ages. Jesus, the son of Sirach, for instance, declares that *He that telleth a tale to a fool speaketh to one in slumber: when he hath told his tale, he will say, What is the matter?*[1] And Hamlet says, *A knavish speech sleeps in a fool's ear.*[2] And Goethe is of the same opinion, that a dull ear mocks at the wisest word,

---

[1]Ecclesiasticus, xxii., 8.
[2]Act iv., sc. 2.

> Das glücklichste Wort es wird verhöhnt,
> Wenn der Hörer ein Schiefohr ist:

and again, that we should not be discouraged if people are stupid, for
you can make no rings if you throw your stone into a marsh:—

> Du wirkest nicht, Alles bleibt so stumpf:
> > Sei guter Dinge!
> Der Stein in Sumpf
> > Macht keine Ringe.

Lichtenberg asks: *When a head and a book come into collision, and one
sounds hollow, is it always the book?* And in another place: *Works like
this are as a mirror: if an ass looks in, you cannot expect an apostle to
look out.* We should do well to remember old Gellert's fine and touching lament, that the best gifts of all find the fewest admirers, and that
most men mistake the bad for the good,—a daily evil that nothing can
prevent, like a plague which no remedy can cure. There is but one
thing to be done, though how difficult!—the foolish must become
wise,—and that they can never be. The value of life they never know;
they see with the outer eye but never with the mind, and praise the trivial because the good is strange to them:—

> Nie kennen sie den Werth der Dinge,
> > Ihr Auge schliesst, nicht ihr Verstand;
> Sie loben ewig das Geringe
> > Weil sie das Gute nie gekannt.

To the intellectual incapacity which, as Goethe says, fails to recog-
nize and appreciate the good which exists, must be added something
which comes into play everywhere, the moral baseness of mankind,
here taking the form of envy. The new fame that a man wins raises him
afresh over the heads of his fellows, who are thus degraded in proportion. All conspicuous merit is obtained at the cost of those who possess
none; or, as Goethe has it in the *West östlicher Divan*, another's praise
is one's own depreciation—

> Wenn wir Andern Ehre geben
> Müssen wir uns selbst entadeln.

We see, then, how it is that, whatever be the form which excellence
takes, mediocrity, the common lot of by far the greatest number, is
leagued against it in a conspiracy to resist, and if possible, to suppress
it. The pass-word of this league is *À bas le mérite.* Nay more; those who
have done something themselves, and enjoy a certain amount of fame,
do not care about the appearance of a new reputation, because its success is apt to throw theirs into the shade. Hence, Goethe declares that

if we had to depend for our life upon the favour of others, we should never have lived at all; from their desire to appear important themselves, people gladly ignore our very existence: —

> Hätte ich gezaudert zu werden,
> Bis man mir's Leben gegönnt,
> Ich wäre noch nicht auf Erden,
> Wie ihr begreifen könnt,
> Wenn ihr seht, wie sie sich geberden,
> Die, um etwas zu scheinen,
> Mich gerne möchten verneinen.

Honour, on the contrary, generally meets with fair appreciation, and is not exposed to the onslaught of envy; nay, every man is credited with the possession of it until the contrary is proved. But fame has to be won in despite of envy, and the tribunal which awards the laurel is composed of judges biassed against the applicant from the very first. Honour is something which we are able and ready to share with everyone; fame suffers encroachment and is rendered more unattainable in proportion as more people come by it. Further, the difficulty of winning fame by any given work stands in inverse ratio to the number of people who are likely to read it; and hence it is so much harder to become famous as the author of a learned work than as a writer who aspires only to amuse. It is hardest of all in the case of philosophical works, because the result at which they aim is rather vague, and, at the same time, useless from a material point of view. They appeal chiefly to readers who are working on the same lines themselves.

It is clear, then, from what I have said as to the difficulty of winning fame, that those who labour, not out of love for their subject, nor from pleasure in pursuing it, but under the stimulus of ambition, rarely or never leave mankind a legacy of immortal works. The man who seeks to do what is good and genuine, must avoid what is bad, and be ready to defy the opinions of the mob, nay, even to despise it and its misleaders. Hence the truth of the remark, (especially insisted upon by Osorius *de Gloria*), that fame shuns those who seek it, and seeks those who shun it; for the one adapt themselves to the taste of their contemporaries, and the others work in defiance of it.

But, difficult though it be to acquire fame, it is an easy thing to keep it when once acquired. Here, again, fame is in direct opposition to honour, with which everyone is presumably to be accredited. Honour has not to be won; it must only not be lost. But there lies the difficulty! For by a single unworthy action, it is gone irretrievably. But fame, in the proper sense of the word, can never disappear; for the action or work by which it was acquired can never be undone; and fame attaches to its author, even though he does nothing to deserve it anew. The fame which vanishes, or is outlived, proves itself thereby to have been spurious, in other words, unmerited, and due to a momentary over-estimate of a man's work; not to speak of the kind of fame which Hegel enjoyed, and which Lichtenberg describes as *trumpeted forth by a clique of admiring undergraduates—the resounding echo of empty heads;—such a fame as will make posterity smile when it lights upon a grotesque architecture of words, a fine nest with the birds long ago flown; it will knock at the door of this decayed structure of convention-alities and find it utterly empty!—not even a trace of thought there to invite the passer-by.*

The truth is that fame means nothing but what a man is in compar-ison with others. It is essentially relative in character, and therefore only indirectly valuable; for it vanishes the moment other people be-come what the famous man is. Absolute value can be predicated only of what a man possesses under any and all circumstances,—here, what a man is directly and in himself. It is the possession of a great heart or a great head, and not the mere fame of it, which is worth having, and conducive to happiness. Not fame, but that which deserves to be fa-mous, is what a man should hold in esteem. This is, as it were, the true underlying substance, and fame is only an accident, affecting its sub-ject chiefly as a kind of external symptom, which serves to confirm his own opinion of himself. Light is not visible unless it meets with some-thing to reflect it; and talent is sure of itself only when its fame is noised abroad. But fame is not a certain symptom of merit; because you can have the one without the other; or, as Lessing nicely puts it, *Some peo-ple obtain fame, and others deserve it.*

It would be a miserable existence which should make its value or want of value depend upon what other people think; but such would be the life of a hero or a genius if its worth consisted in fame, that is, in the applause of the world. Every man lives and exists on his own ac-count, and, therefore, mainly in and for himself; and what he is and the whole manner of his being concern himself more than anyone else; so if he is not worth much in this respect, he cannot be worth much oth-erwise. The idea which other people form of his existence is something secondary, derivative, exposed to all the chances of fate, and in the end affecting him but very indirectly. Besides, other people's heads are a wretched place to be the home of a man's true happiness—a fanciful happiness perhaps, but not a real one.

And what a mixed company inhabits the Temple of Universal Fame!—generals, ministers, charlatans, jugglers, dancers, singers, mil-lionaires and Jews! It is a temple in which more sincere recognition, more genuine esteem, is given to the several excellences of such folk, than to superiority of mind, even of a high order, which obtains from the great majority only a verbal acknowledgment.

From the point of view of human happiness, fame is, surely, nothing but a very rare and delicate morsel for the appetite that feeds on pride and vanity—an appetite which, however carefully concealed, exists to an immoderate degree in every man, and is, perhaps, strongest of all in those who set their hearts on becoming famous at any cost. Such people generally have to wait some time in uncertainty as to their own value, before the opportunity comes which will put it to the proof and let other people see what they are made of; but until then, they feel as if they were suffering secret injustice.[1]

But, as I explained at the beginning of this chapter, an unreasonable value is set upon other people's opinion, and one quite disproportionate to its real worth. Hobbes has some strong remarks on this subject; and no doubt he is quite right. *Mental pleasure,* he writes, *and ecstasy of any kind, arise when, on comparing ourselves with others, we come to the conclusion that we may think well of ourselves.* So we can easily understand the great value which is always attached to fame, as worth any sacrifices if there is the slightest hope of attaining it.

> Fame is the spur that the clear spirit doth raise
> (That last infirmity of noble mind)
> To scorn delights and live laborious days.[2]

And again:

> How hard it is to climb
> The heights where Fame's proud temple shines afar!

We can thus understand how it is that the vainest people in the world are always talking about *la gloire,* with the most implicit faith in it as a stimulus to great actions and great works. But there can be no doubt that fame is something secondary in its character, a mere echo or reflection—as it were, a shadow or symptom—of merit; and, in any case, what excites admiration must be of more value than the admiration itself. The truth is that a man is made happy, not by fame, but by that which brings him fame, by his merits, or to speak more correctly, by the disposition and capacity from which his merits proceed, whether they be moral or intellectual. The best side of a man's nature must of necessity be more important for him than for anyone else: the reflection

---

[1] Our greatest pleasure consists in being admired; but those who admire us, even if they have every reason to do so, are slow to express their sentiments. Hence he is the happiest man who, no matter how, manages sincerely to admire himself—so long as other people leave him alone.

[2] Milton. *Lycidas.*

of it, the opinion which exists in the heads of others, is a matter that can affect him only in a very subordinate degree. He who deserves fame without getting it possesses by far the more important element of happiness, which should console him for the loss of the other. It is not that a man is thought to be great by masses of incompetent and often infatuated people, but that he really is great, which should move us to envy his position; and his happiness lies, not in the fact that posterity will hear of him, but that he is the creator of thoughts worthy to be treasured up and studied for hundreds of years.

Besides, if a man has done this, he possesses something which cannot be wrested from him; and, unlike fame, it is a possession dependent entirely upon himself. If admiration were his chief aim, there would be nothing in him to admire. This is just what happens in the case of false, that is, unmerited, fame; for its recipient lives upon it without actually possessing the solid substratum of which fame is the outward and visible sign. False fame must often put its possessor out of conceit with himself; for the time may come when, in spite of the illusions born of self-love, he will feel giddy on the heights which he was never meant to climb, or look upon himself as spurious coin; and in the anguish of threatened discovery and well-merited degradation, he will read the sentence of posterity on the foreheads of the wise—like a man who owes his property to a forged will.

The truest fame, the fame that comes after death, is never heard of by its recipient; and yet he is called a happy man. His happiness lay both in the possession of those great qualities which won him fame, and in the opportunity that was granted him of developing them—the leisure he had to act as he pleased, to dedicate himself to his favourite pursuits. It is only work done from the heart that ever gains the laurel.

Greatness of soul, or wealth of intellect, is what makes a man happy—intellect, such as, when stamped on its productions, will receive the admiration of centuries to come,—thoughts which made him happy at the time, and will in their turn be a source of study and delight to the noblest minds of the most remote posterity. The value of posthumous fame lies in deserving it; and this is its own reward. Whether works destined to fame attain it in the lifetime of their author is a chance affair, of no very great importance. For the average man has no critical power of his own, and is absolutely incapable of appreciating the difficulty of a great work. People are always swayed by authority; and where fame is widespread, it means that ninety-nine out of a hundred take it on faith alone. If a man is famed far and wide in his own life-time, he will, if he is wise, not set too much value upon it, because it is no more than the echo of a few voices, which the chance of a day has touched in his favour.

Would a musician feel flattered by the loud applause of an audience if he knew that they were nearly all deaf, and that, to conceal their infirmity, they set to work to clap vigorously as soon as ever they saw one or two persons applauding? And what would he say if he got to know that those one or two persons had often taken bribes to secure the loudest applause for the poorest player!

It is easy to see why contemporary praise so seldom developes into posthumous fame. D'Alembert, in an extremely fine description of the temple of literary fame, remarks that the sanctuary of the temple is inhabited by the great dead, who during their life had no place there, and by a very few living persons, who are nearly all ejected on their death. Let me remark, in passing, that to erect a monument to a man in his lifetime is as much as declaring that posterity is not to be trusted in its judgment of him. If a man does happen to see his own true fame, it can very rarely be before he is old, though there have been artists and musicians who have been exceptions to this rule, but very few philosophers. This is confirmed by the portraits of people celebrated by their works; for most of them are taken only after their subjects have attained celebrity, generally depicting them as old and grey; more especially if philosophy has been the work of their lives. From a eudæmonistic standpoint, this is a very proper arrangement; as fame and youth are too much for a mortal at one and the same time. Life is such a poor business that the strictest economy must be exercised in its good things. Youth has enough and to spare in itself, and must rest content with what it has. But when the delights and joys of life fall away in old age, as the leaves from a tree in autumn, fame buds forth opportunely, like a plant that is green in winter. Fame is, as it were, the fruit that must grow all the summer before it can be enjoyed at Yule. There is no greater consolation in age than the feeling of having put the whole force of one's youth into works which still remain young.

Finally, let us examine a little more closely the kinds of fame which attach to various intellectual pursuits; for it is with fame of this sort that my remarks are more immediately concerned.

I think it may be said broadly that the intellectual superiority it denotes consists in forming theories, that is, new combinations of certain facts. These facts may be of very different kinds; but the better they are known, and the more they come within everyday experience, the greater and wider will be the fame which is to be won by theorising about them. For instance, if the facts in question are numbers or lines or special branches of science, such as physics, zoology, botany, anatomy, or corrupt passages in ancient authors, or undecipherable inscriptions, written, it may be, in some unknown alphabet, or obscure points in history; the kind of fame which may be obtained by correctly manipulating such facts will not extend much beyond those who make a study of them—a small number of persons, most of whom live retired lives and are envious of others who become famous in their special branch of knowledge.

But if the facts be such as are known to everyone, for example, the fundamental characteristics of the human mind or the human heart, which are shared by all alike, or the great physical agencies which are constantly in operation before our eyes, or the general course of natural laws, the kind of fame which is to be won by spreading the light of a new and manifestly true theory in regard to them, is such as in time will extend almost all over the civilised world: for if the facts be such as everyone can grasp, the theory also will be generally intelligible. But the extent of the fame will depend upon the difficulties overcome; and the more generally known the facts are, the harder it will be to form a theory that shall be both new and true; because a great many heads will have been occupied with them, and there will be little or no possibility of saying anything that has not been said before.

On the other hand, facts which are not accessible to everybody, and can be got at only after much difficulty and labour, nearly always admit of new combinations and theories; so that, if sound understanding and judgment are brought to bear upon them—qualities which do not involve very high intellectual power—a man may easily be so fortunate as to light upon some new theory in regard to them which shall be also true. But fame won on such paths does not extend much beyond those who possess a knowledge of the facts in question. To solve problems of this sort requires, no doubt, a great deal of study and labour, if only to get at the facts; whilst on the path where the greatest and most widespread fame is to be won, the facts may be grasped without any labour at all. But just in proportion as less labour is necessary, more talent or genius is required; and between such qualities and the drudgery of research no comparison is possible, in respect either of their intrinsic value, or of the estimation in which they are held.

And so people who feel that they possess solid intellectual capacity and a sound judgment, and yet cannot claim the highest mental powers, should not be afraid of laborious study; for by its aid they may work themselves above the great mob of humanity who have the facts constantly before their eyes, and reach those secluded spots which are accessible to learned toil. For this is a sphere where there are infinitely fewer rivals, and a man of only moderate capacity may soon find an opportunity of proclaiming a theory that shall be both new and true; nay, the merit of his discovery will partly rest upon the difficulty of coming at the facts. But applause from one's fellow-students, who are the only persons with a knowledge of the subject, sounds very faint to the far-off multitude. And if we follow up this sort of fame far enough, we shall at last come to a point where facts very difficult to get at are in themselves sufficient to lay a foundation of fame, without any necessity for forming a theory;—travels, for instance, in remote and little-known countries, which make a man famous by what he has seen, not by what he has thought. The great advantage of this kind of fame is that to relate what one has seen, is much easier than to impart one's thoughts, and people are apt to understand descriptions better than ideas, reading the one more readily than the other; for, as Asmus says,

> When one goes forth a-voyaging
> He has a tale to tell.

And yet, for all that, a personal acquaintance with celebrated travellers often reminds us of a line from Horace—new scenes do not always mean new ideas—

> Coelum non animum mutant qui trans mare currunt.[1]

But if a man finds himself in possession of great mental faculties, such as alone should venture on the solution of the hardest of all problems—those which concern nature as a whole and humanity in its widest range, he will do well to extend his view equally in all directions, without ever straying too far amid the intricacies of various by-paths, or invading regions little known; in other words, without occupying himself with special branches of knowledge, to say nothing of their petty details. There is no necessity for him to seek out subjects difficult of access, in order to escape a crowd of rivals; the common objects of life will give him material for new theories at once serious and true; and the service he renders will be appreciated by all those—and they form a great part of mankind—who know the facts of which he treats. What a vast distinction there is between students of physics, chemistry, anatomy, mineralogy, zoology, philology, history, and the men who deal with the great facts of human life, the poet and the philosopher!

---

[1]Epist. I. II.